T0290464

TEXTILE COLLECTIONS

ABOUT THE SERIES
The American Association for State and Local History Book Series addresses issues critical to the field of state and local history through interpretive, intellectual, scholarly, and educational texts. To submit a proposal or manuscript to the series, please request proposal guidelines from AASLH headquarters: AASLH Editorial Board, 1717 Church St., Nashville, Tennessee 37203. Telephone: (615) 320-3203. Website: www.aaslh.org.

ABOUT THE ORGANIZATION
The American Association for State and Local History (AASLH) is a national history membership association headquartered in Nashville, Tennessee. AASLH provides leadership and support for its members who preserve and interpret state and local history in order to make the past more meaningful to all Americans. AASLH members are leaders in preserving, researching, and interpreting traces of the American past to connect the people, thoughts, and events of yesterday with the creative memories and abiding concerns of people, communities, and our nation today. In addition to sponsorship of this book series, AASLH publishes *History News* magazine, a newsletter, technical leaflets and reports, and other materials; confers prizes and awards in recognition of outstanding achievement in the field; supports a broad education program and other activities designed to help members work more effectively; and advocates on behalf of the discipline of history. To join AASLH, go to www.aaslh.org or contact Membership Services, AASLH, 1717 Church St., Nashville, TN 37203.

TEXTILE COLLECTIONS

Preservation, Access, Curation, and Interpretation in the Digital Age

AMANDA GRACE SIKARSKIE

ROWMAN & LITTLEFIELD
Lanham • Boulder • New York • London

Published by Rowman & Littlefield
A wholly owned subsidiary of The Rowman & Littlefield Publishing Group, Inc.
4501 Forbes Boulevard, Suite 200, Lanham, Maryland 20706
www.rowman.com

Unit A, Whitacre Mews, 26-34 Stannary Street, London SE11 4AB

British Library Cataloguing in Publication Information Available

Library of Congress Cataloging-in-Publication Data
Names: Sikarskie, Amanda Grace, 1982– author.
Title: Textile collections : preservation, access, curation, and
   interpretation in the digital age / Amanda Grace Sikarskie.
Description: Lanham : Rowman & Littlefield, [2016] | Series: American
   Association for State and Local History book series | Includes
   bibliographical references and index.
Identifiers: LCCN 2015046400| ISBN 9781442263642 (cloth : alk. paper) | ISBN
   9781442263659 (pbk. : alk. paper)
Subjects: LCSH: Textile museums. | Textile fabrics. | Museum techniques.
Classification: LCC NK8801.8 .S55 2016 | DDC 746.075—dc23 LC record available at
http://lccn.loc.gov/2015046400

Printed in the United States of America

To Ada Lovelace,
the original digital weaver

CONTENTS

LIST OF ILLUSTRATIONS   IX

PREFACE   XI

ACKNOWLEDGMENTS   XV

INTRODUCTION: ADA LOVELACE AND WEAVING THE DIGITAL   1

CHAPTER 1
PRESERVATION   11

CHAPTER 2
ACCESS   43

CHAPTER 3
CURATION   77

CHAPTER 4
INTERPRETATION   107

CHAPTER 5
POSTSCRIPT: MEDITATIONS ON KATE MIDDLETON'S WEDDING DRESS   139

BIBLIOGRAPHY   145

INDEX   155

ABOUT THE AUTHOR   161

Illustrations

Figure I.1.   Silk, Lyons, France   3

Figure I.2.   Jacquard loom   4

Figure I.3.   Ada, Countess of Lovelace   5

Figure 1.1.   *But I Know Crazy* quilt by Luke Haynes   12

Figure 1.2.   Screenshot of the Quilt Index main page   12

Figure 1.3.   Faded claret dye on a quilt from the 1880s   20

Figure 1.4.   Shattering   22

Figure 1.5.   Basic Quilt Index record for *Vanne Pique Fest Onee Rouge*   28

Figure 1.6.   AIDS Memorial Quilt, NAMES Project   37

Figure 2.1.   Christopher Dresser reptilian fabric for the African market   47

Figure 2.2.   Print combining geometric and floral motifs   52

Figure 2.3.   Devoré in polyester   53

Figure 3.1.   Polyvore collection: "Audrey Hepburn on the Moon"   78

Figure 3.2.   Polyvore collection: "The Byzantine Look"   83

Figure 3.3.   Halston Ultrasuede shirtdress   88

Figure 3.4.   Halston and Yves Saint Laurent pajama sets   89

Figure 3.5.   Halston evening ensemble in purple cashmere   90

Figure 4.1.   Chain stitch embroidery and false quilting on a women's dress bodice   114

Figure 4.2.   Chessie Kitten   116

Figure 4.3.   Berlin wool work sampler   124

Figure 4.4.   Berlin wool work slippers   125

Figure 4.5.   The Bon Marché   131

Figure 4.6.   Lanvin frock illustrated in the *Baltimore and Ohio Employees Magazine*   134

Figure 5.1.   Replica of Kate Middleton's wedding dress   140

Preface

THE TERM *TEXTILES* REFERS TO ANY TYPE of cloth or fabric. In practice, *textiles* is a broad, umbrella term that people employ when referring to woven and nonwoven (such as knit or lace) fabrics, including manners of construction (such as the sewing of garments or domestics such as quilts), as well as modes of coloration from dyeing and printing, and finally to needlework techniques and other embellishments such as appliqué and embroidery.[1]

Textile fabrics can be made from a variety of thin, flexible fibers—cotton, wool, silk, or one of the myriad synthetics including nylon, polyester and acrylic, and the like—twisted into yarns and fashioned into fabric through methods such as weaving and knitting. Textiles strongly reflect the aesthetics, values, and ways of life of the cultures that produce them and, as such, make for fascinating objects of study in historical and anthropological collections.

One may well wonder what such warm, fuzzy (and, quite often, pretty) objects have to do with the digital age and why I have chosen to explore *textiles* in digital collections when I could have chosen any other type of object. My own background in the subject is the short explanation—as a textile historian, educator, museum practitioner, and blogger, I have worked with several of the collections profiled in this book, including the Quilt Index and the WGBH Media Library and Archives. More important, however, the intersection of textiles and the digital is, as I will argue in the pages of this book, an important theoretical construct and point of reference not only because of the myriad ways that museum professionals, archivists, artists, and others are creating, preserving, sharing, curating, and interpreting digital textiles but also because of the intimate historical connection between textiles and technology.

Back in 2008, I was working as a graduate research assistant at the Quilt Index, an online archive of quilt images and stories run out of Michigan State University. Chief among my many tasks was the double-checking of database crosswalks, spreadsheet documents that provided detailed instructions for the automated dump of quilt-related metadata from a museum's database into KORA, the index's content management system. After a few weeks of this, I began to take frequent breaks in between the columns of data and allowed my mind to wander. It occurred to me in one of these musing sessions that textiles are a lot like computers—they have the same binary logic.

About This Book

Today, quite innovative things are being done with textile collections online, but this has not been adequately reflected in the publishing world; all we see of these collections are coffee-table books and collections care manuals. *Textile Collections* grew out of the idea that many museum professionals out there—and not only those working in textile collections—would be interested to discover how these very tactile collections are preserved, accessed, curated, and interpreted online, as well as the implications that this work has for current debates in the museum field, such as participatory culture versus curatorial authority and the continuing gender bias in the museum field.

Taking the work of nineteenth-century digital theorist Ada Lovelace as an inspiration and a point of reference, this book utilizes four case studies to explore some of the myriad ways that digital technologies are positively impacting work with historic textile collections. To understand this book in context, I think it is important to note that I myself am active in the textile culture in online worlds. Indeed, each of the chapters of this book is highly personal to me, exploring the collections and websites on which I cut my teeth, so to speak, as a textile historian. Born as Generation X ended and the Millennial generation began, simultaneously an online gamer and blogger *and* a textile historian and educator, it is my hope that my experiences in this liminal *fiberspace*[2] will help to fill the gap between online youth culture and material culture.

Chapter 1, "Preservation," examines an online repository of quilt collections, Michigan State University's Quilt Index, and the ways that repositories of thematic material culture collections facilitate the preservation of both the original, analog object and the images, stories, and other metadata that make up the object's digital surrogate. In chapter 2, "Access," I use various collections from the massive Flickr Commons to Tapestry, an online collection of over four thousand historic fabric swatches at the Design Center at Philadelphia University, to illustrate ways in which new technologies, such as visual stylometry, can be used in the near future to improve users' access by facilitating visual, rather than text-based, searches of collections. Since artificial-intelligence-based visual stylometry is still a few years away for museum collections, chapter 2 also explores how contemporary tools, such as social tagging, can improve access to collections today.

Chapter 3, "Curation," is the only of the four case studies that is not situated around a museum or archival collection. Rather than offering advice for using digital media to bolster the curatorial voice, chapter 3 shines a light on how members of the general public are curating their own collections of historic and history-inspired dress and textiles on social sites such as Polyvore and Tumblr. Through a close reading of authors from such disparate fields as museum studies, sociology, and the philosophy of technology, I hope to persuade the reader that this transfer of some curatorial authority to the public is ultimately a good thing! Finally, chapter 4, "Interpretation," proposes a role for scholars to play in this user-generated, digital world through a case study of my own work in interpreting *Erica*, a needlework instruction program from the 1970s starring embroidery guru Erica Wilson, recently digitized by the WGBH Boston Media Library and Archives as part of an online, open-access initiative.

Threads (pardon the pun) running through all of these case studies are the role of the digital in the democratization of the display of art museum collections and the role that dress[3] and textile collections are currently playing in creating and promoting greater gender equity online. The postscript to this book surveys a recent and infamous example of the latter: the reluctance on the part of *Wikipedia* to allow the creation of an entry on Kate Middleton's wedding dress. Designed by Sarah Burton of Alexander McQueen and embroidered by students and teachers from the Royal School of Needlework, the dress is arguably one of the most historically significant pieces of costume of the early twenty-first century. That preserving its history online could cause such controversy should make even the most Luddite reader call for digital preservation, access, curation, and interpretation of their institution's collections.

While much of the information contained within these pages is directed toward those who manage historic dress or textile collections on a day-to-day basis, this book is really intended for anyone who loves textiles—museum curators and educators, conservators, and even design-ers, makers, and collectors. After all, as Ada Lovelace so eloquently noted back in the nineteenth century, textiles *are* digital. Their simple, yet elegant, logic of interlocking yarns made computers—and their sundry applications—possible. And it all started with warp and weft.

Notes

1. Kathryn L. Hatch, *Textile Science* (Minneapolis-Saint Paul: West Publishing, 1993), 7–13.

2. The term *fiberspace*, as used in this context, comes from my doctoral dis-sertation, "Fiberspace" (Michigan State University, 2011), which attempted to describe the online spaces in which computer culture and quilter-knitter-crafter culture mixed, including quilt shops in the virtual world *Second Life* and tailoring and other crafting professions in the massively multiplayer online role-playing game *World of Warcraft*.

3. Throughout this book, the term *dress* is generally used, rather than *costume* or *apparel* or *fashion*. *Dress* tends to be the preferred term among academics in the British Isles, while *costume* has traditionally been the term used by American historians. In light of recent discussions within the Costume Society of America on changing its own name to the Dress Society, Fashion Society, or something similar, I have opted for the term *dress* for two main reasons: *Dress* is less likely to be confusing to people outside the discipline than *costume*, which can conjure up images of theatrical costumes for the general reader. And unlike *fashion*, which implies only those aspects of dress that are or were fashion*able*, *dress* feels like a broader umbrella term.

Acknowledgments

FIRST OF ALL, A BIG THANK YOU to Charles Harmon and Robert Hayunga at Rowman & Littlefield. You were both so easy to work with and made the experience of writing my first academic book remarkably low stress. Thanks also to Janneken Smucker; Marsha MacDowell and Mary Worrall of the Quilt Index and Michigan State University Museum; Allison Pekel, my project manager at the WGBH Media Library and Archives; and the Mellon Foundation, the American Quilt Study Group, and the Visual Resources Association, for funding research projects and presentations that later became a part of this larger *Textile Collections* book. Finally, many thanks to the Los Angeles County Museum of Art for donating to the public domain many of the photographs of textiles and historic dress used as illustrations in this book. Such generosity makes access to these and other historic art forms possible.

Introduction
Ada Lovelace and Weaving the Digital

T HE LOOM, LIKE THE COMPUTER, uses a binary code for processing infinitely complex information. Warp and weft, zero and one share a common language. So much of our everyday understanding of culture comes from the construction of binaries:

hard versus soft
cool versus warm
masculine versus feminine

These binary oppositions represent computing and textiles, respectively, in the popular imagination, with computers being seen as cool, hard, sleek, and the preserve of men, whereas textiles are culturally constructed as soft and warm, fuzzy, feminine, motherly. In thinking through these binaries for the first time, I thought I had hit upon some tremendous revelation, but I quickly discovered that I had been beaten to the idea by nearly 175 years.

This linkage between digital technology and the textile arts, especially weaving, was first articulated in the work of the mathematician Ada, Countess of Lovelace, and her technical and theoretical writings of the punch cards of the Jacquard loom in the programming of the first proto-computer. While much has been written by scholars of computer history and contemporary digital culture, such as James Essinger and Howard Rheingold, on the contribution of weaving—specifically, the contribution of Jacquard loom punch cards—to the development of computing and information processing, and published studies in the fields of textiles and contemporary art document digitally assisted weaving practices today, little work has been done placing the one in the context of the other.

Weaving, very simply, is the practice of interlocking two strands of yarn, the warp and weft, at right angles to form a material, such as cloth. The coarser the yarn, the easier it is to handle. Fine, delicate fibers, such as silk, are more difficult to work with, and places of woven textile manufacturing became not only economic centers of activity but also centers of artistic creativity and technical skill. The French city of Lyons and the London neighborhood of Spitalfields, for instance, were renowned for their intricately patterned woven silk production by the end of the eighteenth century. The changing fashions of the day created a problem for the industry, though, in that a loom was built to weave one particular pattern—say, a rose-patterned brocade (see figure I.1). When a pattern (let us continue with the example of roses) went out of fashion in Paris or London society, the demand for that cloth declined, new punch cards had to be created, the loom had to be rethreaded, and the dobby head or the Jacquard mechanism had to be reset in order to create a new pattern.[1]

Joseph Marie Jacquard, a Lyonnais weaver working at the beginning of the nineteenth century, famously asked, "What do you do when roses go out of fashion?" and sought to improve the productivity of the city's silk industry by creating a *programmable* loom, a loom that could be programmed through the use of punched cards to weave sundry different patterns while keeping its basic machinery intact. In computing terms, the punch cards for the patterns to be woven functioned as the software on this loom, while the machinery, the loom itself, was the hardware. The Jacquard loom, invented in 1801, was thus one of the first, perhaps the first, computers ever built. Computing as we know it was necessitated by the manufacture of textiles. That the first computer was a loom for the weaving of silk brocade stands in stark contrast to both the vision of textiles as women's "gentle arts" and the vision of computers as sleek, futuristic, and masculine.

Prior to the nineteenth century, the word *computer* had quite a different meaning, simply "one who computes." The word had been in use since the seventeenth century, but, significantly, by the nineteenth century, it was applied to women who did calculation work for insurance companies, nautical and astronomical charts, and other organizations dealing with large amounts of figures. Women *were* computers, and one woman who longed to be a computer, despite (or perhaps because of) her privileged background, was Ada Lovelace.

Ada, Countess of Lovelace, née Ada Byron, was the daughter of Romantic poet Lord Byron and Annabella, Lady Byron, very much a child of the Enlightenment. Or rather, as Lovelace biographer Benjamin Woolley

Figure I.1.   Silk, Lyons, France, circa 1730–1750. Los Angeles County Museum of Art collection.

Figure I.2.   Jacquard loom. Photo by John R. Southern. Ontario Science Centre collection.

has suggested, she was the daughter of Romanticism and Reason themselves.[2] Put another way, Ada Lovelace, in terms of both her own personal
history and the early Victorian era in which she lived, an era that saw the
rise of the first truly modern technologies, embodies many of the binary
tensions described in the first pages of this book. Like that which stands at
the intersection of textiles and technology today, Lovelace was at once the
scientific, the technological, the cool, the masculine, and the poetic, the
Romantic, the warm, the fuzzy, the feminine.

Lovelace's short life (she died at the age of thirty-six) was marked by
her love of mathematics and calculating technologies, but also by an es-
trangement from her father from infancy, a gambling addiction, numerous
extramarital affairs, a general ambivalence toward her aristocratic husband
and their three children, and numerous health problems, including frequent migraine headaches, anxiety and panic attacks, and uterine problems,
eventually diagnosed as the cancer that took her life. Lady Byron wrote
that Ada's numerous health problems were due to her "overexcitement"
and too much thinking about mathematics, while Lovelace herself saw
something insidious in the transitional age in which she lived, citing "the
high pressure of the present age & epoch & state of society" as the root
cause of her suffering.[3]

Figure I.3. Ada, Countess of Lovelace. Collection of the National Portrait Gallery, London.

Lovelace is known today for her collaboration with inventor Charles Babbage, especially her writings that theorized Babbage's work, and for her translation and extensive notes on a paper by the French scientist L. F. Menabrea, "Sketch of the Analytical Engine Invented by Charles Babbage." It is not insignificant that Ada Lovelace was aware of and fascinated by Jacquard's loom some years before Charles Babbage had considered the use of the punch cards from the loom in the programming of the Analytical Engine. On a trip through industrial north England in the summer of 1834, Ada and her mother, Lady Byron, saw the looms in action, and Lady Byron created a drawing of the punch card used in the weaving of ribbons.[4] "Ada was particularly sensitive to the significance of the Jacquard loom in Babbage's plans. The best way to understand her contribution to Babbage's work is to see it in terms of the relationship between Babbage's work and Jacquard's. Ada loved the Jacquard loom, and added it to her many scientific fascinations."[5] Lovelace's position, then, as what one could call the world's first software developer, was a bringing together, through languages, both literary and binary, of the spheres of computing and textiles. Lovelace wrote of the Analytical Engine,

> The distinctive characteristic of the Analytical Engine, and that which has rendered it possible to endow mechanism with such extensive facilities as bid fair to make this engine the executive right-hand of abstract algebra, is the introduction into it of the principle which Jacquard devised for regulating, by means of punched cards, the most complicated patterns in the fabrication of brocaded stuffs. It is in this that the distinction between the two engines lies. Nothing of the sort exists in the Difference Engine. We may say most aptly that the Analytical Engine *weaves algebraic patterns* just as the Jacquard-loom weaves flowers and leaves. [Ada's italics][6]

The rather poetic idea of *weaving algebraic patterns*, that mathematical calculations are made up of a binary logic, a warp and a weft that could be woven by a machine into a logical fabric, was an extraordinary one. And it was an idea that formed the basis for the discipline of computer programming.

According to James Essinger, author of *Jacquard's Web: How a Hand-loom Led to the Birth of the Information Age*, Lovelace's great achievement in the field of computer programming was not in the translation of Menabrea's writings on the Analytical Engine, but rather in her own writing on the Analytical Engine in the extensive notes she published along with the translation.

> Had Ada *only* [emphasis in original] translated Menabrea's paper her achievement would have been merely a linguistic one. Furthermore, one could reasonably have said that she was to a large extent translating a paper whose intellectual content was substantially Babbage's own. But in fact Ada's translation was merely the starting-point for her work, for published translation is accompanied by seven additional Notes (she consistently capitalized the word). These, denoted by the letters A to G, extend to more than 20,000 words: that is, about twice as long as the actual translation.

They offer a penetrating insight into the Analytical Engine, with its revolutionary design and objectives and with its intimate conceptual connection
with the Jacquard loom.[7]

In these notes, Lovelace brought together, from both a theoretical and a
practical standpoint, textiles and technology.

Running counter to Lovelace's idea of weaving the digital were the Luddites, the most historically infamous reactionaries against weaving technology
(and perhaps against any technology). A word now applied to any techno-
phobe, the origin of the term *Luddite* comes from the British textile workers,
both men and women, who, around 1810, rose up against their employers
and smashed the new mechanized textile looms.[8] It was not truly the technology to which they objected, however. It was the business philosophies of
industrial capitalism that would allow skilled human beings to be made redun-
dant by machines. Ever since then, however, antitechnological sentiment has
been intimately connected with the textile arts in history as well as language.

Ultimately, it is the Luddite's vision of the Jacquard loom, rather than
the vision of Ada Lovelace, that has become the prevailing narrative of
textiles and technology in the nineteenth century. The ideal of the Cult
of True Womanhood, the Victorian woman as housebound keeper of the
domestic sphere, was an ideal from which Lovelace greatly diverged, and
as such, her work was largely overlooked. Most Victorian women, quite
unlike Lovelace, viewed the mechanized looms with a mixture of fear,
suspicion, and pity. Popular novelists, such as Elizabeth Gaskell in *North
and South* (1854–1855),[9] expressed anxiety, albeit sympathetic, toward in-
dustrialization and the textile mills in the north of England.

It was in the twentieth century that Lovelace's substantial contribution to computing became fully understood, though some scholars were
slow to admit her importance, ascribing much of her work to Babbage.
In his seminal essay, "Computing Machinery and Intelligence" (1950),[10]
Alan Turing anticipated flaws she might have found in his own thinking
on artificial intelligence in a section called "Lady Lovelace's Objection."
In 1979–1980, the computer programming language developed by the
United States Department of Defense was dubbed "Ada." Lovelace's ideas
about binary logic and using punch card programming as "weaving the
digital" have clear connections to computers and computer programming
as they developed in the early and middle twentieth century.

Many scholars also credit Lovelace's ideas about weaving the digital
as the intellectual framework upon which the Internet and World Wide
Web are built as well. For Essinger, "It is not stretching credibility too far

to describe the Internet itself as Jacquard's Web."[11] Similarly, cybertheorist Sadie Plant argues in *Zeros and Ones*[12] that the act of weaving and the World Wide Web are intimately connected, not just because of Lovelace's use of the punch cards of an industrial loom but also because webs are, by nature, woven. For Plant, women are the spiders weaving the World Wide Web. While this kind of logic can push theory into the bounds of ideology, Plant's rhetoric of weaving proves useful for understanding Lovelace's contributions outside the realm of mathematics and computer science. In her essay "Otherwise Unobtainable: The Applied Arts and the Politics and Poetics of Digital Technology," British textile historian Tanya Harrod echoed Plant's arguments over a decade later: "But textiles appear ready for anything, as Sadie Plant points out in *Zeros and Ones*, where Jacquard looms (in any case prophetic of computing) interweave multiple functions: combining software and hardware; displaying cloth as material and an information storage system, as a product and a process."[13] Indeed, there is a great resemblance between the binary logic and actual look of a punch card used in programming in the pixel-based method in which digital images are rendered.

> The pixel-based method of representing an image bears a great resemblance to the way the master-weavers of Lyons wove images from silk. This is because the woven images created in silk fabric by the master-weavers of Lyons on the Jacquard looms still used in Croiz Rousse are themselves in fact nothing more or less than digital images. A digital image in this sense is one in which the picture is represented by a code consisting of only two elements. A digital image is made using a representational system that places images on a grid, with the tiny squares or rectangles of the grid being either filled in with a colour (which may include black or white) or left blank. The "filling in" is one element and the blankness is the other. Those are, by the very nature of weaving and computing, the only two options.[14]

Not only did weaving give rise to computing and the digital, but computing and the digital have also facilitated many changes in the ways in which weavers and other textile artists work, in terms of both form and content.

Regina Cornwell noted, "A hundred years before ENIAC,[15] Ada Lovelace mused about the Analytical Engine as a rich source not only for scientific and mathematical explorations, but also for art and imagination."[16] It is to the role of computing in fostering art and imagination in the fabric arts that we now turn, because although this book focuses almost exclusively on museum practice and the role of textiles in historic collections, it is important, before we begin, to note the degree to which these same ideas and technologies have impacted *artists* and the *creation* of textiles.

British weaver Ann Sutton (b. 1935) pioneered the field of digital textiles, joining the Computer Arts Society in the 1960s. She uses a "programmable dobby loom in which the computer instructs the loom with her design," and for Harrod, "some of the excitement is when the yarns have their say, responding unexpectedly to the cloth."[17] There are also many computing applications for weaving beyond the high-art and strictly digital contexts; individual crafters who weave make use of a variety of digital technologies. Judy Heim's *The Needlecrafter's Computer Companion* (1995) features an entire chapter, "Amazing Feats of Star-Trek-Like Computer Wizardry Involving Yarn," with a section on software for weavers.[18] Software packages for weavers to render designs on their PC include Fiberworks, JaqCAD, Weave, Weavemaker, and Swiftweave (for Macintosh). There are also numerous online discussion networks, social networks, and websites for weavers, spinners, and dyers. Because computing began with weaving, the production of fabric, and the loom, computing is inexorably tied in theory and praxis to textiles, perhaps even more so in the early twenty-first century. It perhaps goes without saying that weaving is not the only textile discipline that has changed and evolved to incorporate digital culture and digital technologies. Every fabric craft—quilting, knitting, sewing, cross-stitch, and beyond—has effectively become a mathematical, digital craft in the early twenty-first century. However, as we have seen, it is crucial to ground the study of the digital in its historical antecedents.

Telling the story of Lovelace and the Jacquard loom, of the shared binary nature of computer programs and woven fabric, gives digital work in textile collections today a historical context and begins to take apart the stereotypes of women and computing, and of women and textiles. The histories of textiles and digital technology have been woven together since the early nineteenth century when Ada, Countess of Lovelace, wrote of the use of the punch cards from the Jacquard weaving loom in the programming of Charles Babbage's protocomputer, the Analytical Engine, as "weaving" numbers and programming. Unsurprisingly, the histories of textiles and the digital are woven together even more tightly in the digital age. Today, digital textiles and other digital material culture raise profound questions for the future of museum practice and object-based academic disciplines.

It is thus important to note the extent to which Ada Lovelace's work informs the history and theory that lie beneath this book. The pages and ideas that follow are, in a small but nonetheless important way, a continuation of Ada Lovelace's ideas and work, which were cut tragically short and whose conceptual significance for the field of textile studies were largely forgotten for around 175 years.

Notes

1. Thanks very much to Patricia Cox Crews, professor emeritus of textiles at the University of Nebraska-Lincoln and founding director of the International Quilt Study Center and Museum, for her explanation of changing the Jacquard loom over from one pattern to another.

2. Benjamin Woolley, *The Bride of Science: Romance, Reason and Byron's Daughter* (London: Macmillan, 1999), 2.

3. Alison Winter, "A Calculus of Suffering: Ada Lovelace and the Bodily Constraints of Women's Knowledge in Early Victorian England," in *Science Incarnate: Historical Embodiments of Natural Knowledge*, eds. Christopher Lawrence and Steven Shapin (Chicago: University of Chicago Press, 1998), 233.

4. James Essinger, *Jacquard's Web: How a Hand-loom Led to the Birth of the Information Age* (Oxford: Oxford University Press, 2004), 138–39.

5. Essinger, 123.

6. Essinger, 141.

7. Essinger, 123.

8. See Stephen Jones's *Against Technology: From the Luddites to Neo-Luddism* for a further historical discussion of the Luddites.

9. Elizabeth Gaskell, *North and South* (London: Oxford University Press, 1973).

10. Alan Turing, "Computing Machinery and Intelligence," *Mind* 59 (1950).

11. Essinger, 257.

12. Sadie Plant, *Zeros and Ones: Digital Women and the New Technoculture* (New York: Doubleday, 1997).

13. Tanya Harrod, "Otherwise Unobtainable: The Applied Arts and the Politics and Poetics of Digital Technology," in *NeoCraft: Modernity and the Crafts*, ed. Sandra Alfoldy (Halifax: Press of the Nova Scotia College of Art and Design, 2007), 235.

14. Essinger, 294.

15. ENIAC was the first electronic general-purpose computer.

16. Regina Cornwell, "From the Analytical Engine to Lady Ada's Art," in *Iterations: The New Image*, ed. Timothy Druckrey (Cambridge, MA: MIT Press, 1993), 51.

17. Harrod, 234.

18. Judy Heim, *The Needlecrafter's Computer Companion* (San Francisco: No Starch Press, 1995).

Preservation 1

AN IMAGE OF SOUL AND FUNK LEGEND James Brown (see figure 1.1) might seem like an unlikely place to begin a survey of the preservation benefits of digital textile collections. This quilted portrait is clearly a contemporary art piece, so surely someone is looking after it, right? As it happens, yes. But since the work resides in private hands, its future preservation is effectively unknowable, and preservation of its digital surrogate becomes especially important.

Digital archives such as the Quilt Index (see figure 1.2) are meeting this critical need, preserving (and shaping) quilt history as it happens, documenting old and new quilts, and safeguarding physical objects and digital surrogates alike. Based at Michigan State University, the Quilt Index,[1] www.quiltindex.org, is a vast online digital repository storing and serving images and metadata for tens of thousands of historic and contemporary quilts.[2] Though the index went live in 2003, it comes out of a lineage of paper-based, largely community-driven quilt documentation projects going back to the 1980s.[3] Today, these digital quilt records are contributed by dozens of institutions throughout the United States and around the world and are not housed in any single location.

> The Quilt Index is, in effect, a digital library, museum, and archive. As a digital archive, it has a repository function, with servers to preserve and maintain the digital image files and metadata descriptions. As a library, the Quilt Index provides access to the entire corpus online, and provides tools for viewing and reading the contributed artifacts. The exhibition function of the Quilt Index presents the objects with context—in relation, comparison, or juxtaposition to other quilts or objects, along with curated material written by researchers.[4]

Figure 1.1. *But I Know Crazy* quilt by Luke Haynes, 2009. Private collection. Courtesy of the owner.

Figure 1.2. Screenshot of the Quilt Index main page. Courtesy of the Quilt Index and the Michigan State University Museum.

Thus, rather than a brick-and-mortar quilt museum, the Quilt Index essentially serves as a virtual clearinghouse for quilt images and metadata.

This chapter explores preservation and how online repositories such as the Quilt Index foster the preservation of both textile objects *and* their digital surrogates. The chapter opens with "What Quilts Get Preserved?," a discussion of the logic and limitations of selecting quilts for documentation and the historical prejudice against machine-made quilts. The next part of this chapter, "Preserving the Material Object," is a brief exploration of some of the ways in which digital collections of textile objects (in this case, quilts) facilitate the preservation of the physical object. Digital surrogates of material culture—images and metadata—present their own unique preservation challenges, however, and using a mix of history, theory, and applied, real-world information, the bulk of the chapter ("Preserving Digital Objects," "Preserving the Textual Record," and "Preserving the Digital Image") discusses the preservation of these digital records and images. Above all, I argue that a good custom metadata scheme is the best bet for a successful digital preservation project.

What Quilts Get Preserved?

Many records and images on the Quilt Index come from museum collections, but many more have come from grassroots, state-level quilt documentation projects. The idea of state-by-state quilt documentation comes straight out of the Bicentennial and the nostalgia for early America that so marked that period, though many of the projects were completed in the 1980s and into the 1990s. Documented in the field on paper forms by volunteers, these projects, while quite democratic in some ways, can be downright exclusionary. Such documentation projects often, but not always, had a "cut-off" date, not recording information about quilts made after, say, 1940 or 1950. The rationale was twofold. First, it is these old quilts that are most fragile and in most need of preservation. Even in a time before the World Wide Web, the organizers of these projects were thinking of quilt documentation as a means by which to foster physical preservation. Second, quilts made after 1940 are much more likely to have been made on a machine and therefore seem to be not as "interesting" to the history buff with a passion for traditional quilts. Thus, for some states, the corpus of quilt data on the Quilt Index is incomplete, skewed to preserve only old quilts. This presents a real preservation problem because, as we have seen, new quilts (as well as old) benefit from digital preservation.

Enter, the Sewing Machine

Of any technological innovation that has changed quilts and quiltmaking, the sewing machine is probably the most obvious. Walter Hunt invented the two-thread interlocked stitch sewing machine in the 1830s, and as Barbara Brackman notes in *Patterns of Progress: Quilts in the Machine Age*, from its very inception, there was speculation that the sewing machine would drastically alter women's lives. According to Brackman, Hunt's daughter was so worried that the popularization of the sewing machine would ruin women across America financially by depriving them of incomes from hand sewing that Hunt never marketed his invention.[5] The sewing machine was reinvented in the 1840s by Elias Howe and marketed to individual households in the United States by Singer beginning in the 1850s. Hunt's fears, however, were unfounded. Rather than making single women destitute, the demonstration and marketing of the sewing machine actually provided many nineteenth-century women with an opportunity for employment outside the home.

This economic opportunity was not the only way in which the sewing machine changed women's lives in the nineteenth century. Dramatically cutting the time required for chore or household sewing, the sewing machine gave many women much more time for "fancy" sewing. The extra time, combined with influences from Japanese design and British illustration exhibited at the 1876 Centennial Exposition in Philadelphia, led to the development and popularity of the crazy quilt in America.

The sewing machine not only changed the way in which women envisioned themselves and their households in the nineteenth century but also changed quilt styles and provided new kinds of employment for women as sewing machine demonstrators and salespeople.[6] In her history of machine quilting, Barbara Brackman noted four major changes to the craft that were brought about by machine sewing: a focus on intricate appliqué, the incorporation of many thin scraps of several very different fabrics (the crazy quilt), a shift from valuing the stitches to valuing the choice and arrangement of fabrics, and, finally, the loss of hand-sewing skills as one of the hallmarks of a genteel young woman.[7]

Besides facilitating the shift in fashion from the block quilt to the crazy quilt, the ways in which women (and men) were using the sewing machine also led to a fashion for multiple borders, allowed for easier use of fancy stitches, and subsequently led to a change in the valuation of quality in quiltmaking. Whereas in the pre–sewing machine period, quality in quilting had largely been judged based upon the quality and evenness of stitches, especially quilting stitches, in the post–sewing machine period of the nineteenth century, quality was judged more upon design and the number and variety of different fabrics used.[8]

Today, computerization of sewing machines makes possible techniques such as digital photo transfer directly onto fabric, as seen in Luke Haynes's quilted portrait of James Brown. In response to a woman at a craft show who "claimed it isn't quilting unless you sew blocks with paper pieces,"[9] Judy Heim has defended the integrity of machine- and computer-aided quilting this way:

> "So why even bother sewing the quilt?" you ask. Why not let the com-
> puter just print a picture of it? Lest you fear, like the woman at the craft
> show, that quilt-making is getting too high-tech, rest assured that beyond
> the initial design stages, the relationship between you and your quilt has
> not changed. You are still guaranteed hundreds of cozy hours with fabric
> piled on your lap and pins falling on the floor. Your cat will still ingest a
> half spool of expensive Mettler thread.[10]

Even in the early twenty-first century, the study of quilts and quilt-making through the lens of technology may seem counterintuitive to many not familiar with the history of quiltmaking in America. "Still, it may seem odd that craftspeople, often engaged in a life-long project of metaphorically 'warming the world' through their work, have in recent years so dedicatedly embraced supposedly 'cold' computers and the communication technology they offer. Remember that in general, technological development has always been regarded as a threat to the crafts."[11] So, to provide a tentative summary, technological innovation has actually had a tremendous impact on quiltmaking—in terms of the visual appearance of quilts, the ways in which quilts were made, and the daily lives of quiltmakers. This reliance on and embracing of the technological, however, seems to fly in the face of quiltmaking in the popular imagination as a pastime rooted not in technology and the new but in tradition, the past, and the handmade.

A Romantic Reaction to Machine Sewing

Artists, designers, and critics, not mill workers, were the true techno-phobes of the Victorian period—so much so, in fact, that today it would be more appropriate to call a technophobic person a "Ruskin" rather than a "Luddite." The Victorians' aesthetic reaction to the marriage of art and science, to mechanized means of production, and to the erosion of the handmade was strong, and this artistic reaction to nineteenth-century science and technology had broad effects upon the visual culture (and perhaps especially the textiles) of not only the Victorian and Edwardian periods but also those of the late twentieth and early twenty-first centuries.

Elizabeth Cumming, in her essay "Pure Magic," notes that "the Arts and Crafts Movement is often seen as a romantic reaction to the Industrial Revolution."[12] Mechanization of industry, mass-production of household goods, and the rapid transition from stone to iron and glass in architecture, while seen as progress to some, seemed like ruination to others, like influential art critic John Ruskin, who used his influence as an arbiter of taste to call for arts that were divorced from machine production. The arts and crafts movement is often dated to 1861, when artist and textile designer William Morris established his studio. Like Ruskin, Morris lamented the mechanization of the arts. His works were produced entirely by hand, using natural dyes rather than the chemical aniline dyes that became widely available around 1860. Morris's works were typically medieval in inspiration, reinterpreting the past as a more ideal, pastoral, and authentic world. Another proponent of the arts and crafts movement, Charles Eastlake, wrote in his influential treatise on interior decoration, *Hints on Household Taste*, "The modern development of art is full of strange inconsistencies, and they are nowhere more apparent than in the connection of design with manufacture."[13] By the late nineteenth century, the arts and crafts movement had great influence on interior design on both sides of the Atlantic—even, ironically, upon mass-produced home furnishings and fabrics.[14]

While the arts and crafts movement had an impact upon ideas about good (read: free of mechanized technology) design more broadly, the related aesthetic movement had a tremendous impact upon quiltmaking. Heavily influenced by the opening of Japan and the subsequent exhibition of Japanese design at the Philadelphia Centennial Exposition of 1876, the aesthetic movement was fascinated by not only the quality and craftsmanship of Japanese decorative arts but also the free use of line and asymmetry. Crazy quilts were inspired by Japanese art and facilitated by the introduction of the sewing machine, which freed up women's time from mending clothing and household textiles and allowed them to concentrate on fancier stitchery. The work of Britain's Royal School of Art and the illustrations of Kate Greenaway were also highly influential upon quilting in the period from roughly 1876 to 1910. The subject matter of such illustrations was reinterpreted into design stamps that could be printed onto fabric at home. This led to a craze for embroidered quilts. As with the fashion for crazy quilting, the art needlework phenomenon was brought about by a simultaneous convergence of the availability of a moderately priced sewing machine for domestic use and the related aesthetic reaction to machine-produced material culture.

Redwork, a form of art needlework in turkey red[15] thread on a white or cream quilted ground, was the most common manifestation of the art needlework craze in quilting in the period. The embroidered designs on redwork quilts were typically whimsical or sentimental, often depicting subjects such as flowers, animals, children, or nursery rhyme characters. These designs were stamped or punched with equipment purchased from mail-order catalogs, and then hand-embroidered onto the quilt top. The sources for the designs were often found in women's periodicals of the day or specialty embroidery design catalogs. Merchandise catalogs were developed in the nineteenth century, playing an important role in the marketing of these new textile arts. Mass-circulated periodicals, funded in large measure by the advertising revenue of department stores[16] and mail-order warehouses, exploded in the middle and late nineteenth century, with numerous titles on fashion and needlework that were aimed at women, including *The Delineator, Godey's Lady's Book, Harper's Bazaar, Ladies' Home Journal,* and *Modern Priscilla.*

Victorian households reacted to the introduction of mass-produced goods and new technologies, such as the sewing machine, into the home by engaging in a collective nostalgia for preindustrial material culture. Books such as Alice Morse Earle's *Home Life in Colonial Days* (1898), Marie Webster's *Quilts: Their Story and How to Make Them* (1915), and Ruth Finley and Ruby McKim's *Old Patchwork Quilts and the Women Who Made Them* (1929) reflected a yearning for an imagined pretechnological American colonial past. Laurel Thatcher Ulrich notes in *The Age of Homespun,*

> In the last half of the nineteenth century, the mystique of homespun spread. It attracted social reformers, as well as conservatives, the arts and crafts movement as well as the colonial revival, and academic artists like Thomas Eakins as well as popular illustrators. By the 1890s, antique spinning wheels were everywhere, even in the mansion of a Montana mining magnate.[17]

Related to the colonial revival in the decorative arts and the broader rejection of machine-assisted means of production in the decorative arts was the disavowal of the utility of the sewing machine. In the April 1870 issue of the *Lady's Friend* magazine, an editorial read, "The sewing machine, like a magician out of fairyland, turns off yards upon yards of flouncing, and ruffling, and fluting, and fureblows generally . . . so that at present it really seems that nothing was gained by this beneficial invention. . . . The labor and weariness of the needle are not abated one bit."[18] The sarcastic tone, describing the sewing machine as "a magician out of fairyland," figures the technology as an otherworldly trickster. Owing to the fact that sewing machine manufacturers and related companies accounted for much of their advertising revenue, such sentiments were perhaps less common in ladies' magazines than those in favor of the sewing machine.[19] As the following example of Sunbonnet Sue illustrates, counterarguments against the sewing machine reflect unease with machine sewing.

The Sun Sets on Sunbonnet Sue

The Sun Sets on Sunbonnet Sue,[20] a quilt created over a century after the invention of the sewing machine, in the midst of the American Bicentennial, another sentimental and patriotic revival, can be read as metaphor for the decline of women's sewing skills in America, as well as a document of technological anxiety. Created by the feminist quilting group the Seamsters Union in Lawrence, Kansas, in 1979, the quilt[21] features several vignettes in which Sunbonnet Sue, a popular pattern in quiltmaking since the late nineteenth century, is killed in creatively macabre fashions, such as being crushed by a falling Skylab and from radiation poisoning from nuclear fallout at Three Mile Island.

The death of Sue is symbolic of the decline of hand sewing and the death of the Cult of True Womanhood. Also known as "The Cult of Domesticity," Barbara Welter writes in "The Cult of True Womanhood: 1820–1860" that the "True Woman" of the mid-nineteenth century was envisioned as being not only pious, pure of heart, and submissive but also highly domestic, upholding the division between the home sphere and the outside world that was simultaneously constructed and threatened by the Industrial Revolution. Further, in each of these two examples, Sue is killed by a technological accident. While humorous in their cartoonish absurdity, the images are nonetheless rather disconcerting. These quilt blocks represent the incursion of futuristic technologies into the realm of the fabric arts and all its associated cultural baggage of tradition, womanhood, the home, handcrafts, and an imagined ideal American past.

Preserving the Material Object

In her seminal lecture, "Preservation of Textile Objects,"[22] Agnes Geijer asked, "How are precious old textiles to be treated—the ones excavated and the ones never buried?"[23] While this book is specifically *not* intended as a volume on collections care, as there are several good works on the subject out already, it is worth noting a bit about the preservation of physical collections here, both as background and because digital collections are instrumental in the long-term preservation of material objects. While there are many types of physical textile objects that specifically benefit from digital preservation, I will discuss two here: works not in museum collections and fragile or degrading works.

Works Not in Museum Collections

How does a quilt in a private collection come into the Quilt Index? Let us return to the example of the James Brown quilt from the beginning of this chapter. *But I Know Crazy*, by West Coast quilt artist Luke Haynes, is one of thousands of quilts on the Quilt Index that is held in a private collection. While the staff at the index are currently working on a mechanism for public submission of quilt records (which would foster not only preservation in this way but also sustainability by creating an income stream), this quilt's image and metadata came into the index in a batch as part of the Quilt Alliance's (then the Alliance for American Quilts) 2009 contest, "Crazy for Quilts." Besides preserving the images of all the quilts included in the contest, the quilt's record also preserves the words of the quiltmaker: "This quilt made itself. With the title of the project I couldn't help thinking of the James Brown quote 'I don't know Karate . . . But I Know Crazy.' Having laughed at that line every time it came up in the song, it made an association for me with the word crazy. When Amy [Milne, executive director of the Quilt Alliance] told me of the crazy quilts contest, it just made sense. I also played with new methods here."[24] While this privately held quilt was submitted to the index by an organization, the Quilt Alliance, the preservation potential for user-submitted quilt records is enormous. In 2009, the Quilt Index piloted public individual submission of quilt records through the Signature Quilt Project.[25] While the project resulted in the submission of over sixty quilt records, the tremendous staff time required to train the public in metadata generation and to troubleshoot difficulties with metadata entry means that, for now, there are still several practical and technical issues that continue to make a broader democratization of projects such as this problematic.

Fragile or Degrading Works

There are, of course, many causes for the fragility of the textile object. Wear and handling, soil, damage from pests, fungus, and other microorganisms, or water, improper storage—in terms of either an acid environment or poor or irregular hanging or folding—and improper cleaning are all major causes of fragility and decay of textile fabrics.[26] Light is often the major culprit, however, and light is, unfortunately, a necessity in the brick-and-mortar museum gallery.

Light plays a predominant role. . . . Light not only fades colours but also intensifies the oxidizing process in the fibres, thus promoting their destruction. The preservation of colours raises very intricate problems. It is indeed difficult to reconcile the need for protection against the harmful effects of light with the legitimate desire of museums to exhibit the objects at their best to the public. Unfortunately the manner of displaying textiles in our museums often constitutes a direct danger to them.[27]

Sometimes, however, even the best preservation history will not have saved a textile from fragility. Dyes are a primary offender in this area.

In 1856, teenage chemist William Henry Perkin accidentally synthesized the first synthetic dye—mauve.[28] Before then, all dyes were natural, made from fruits, roots, flowers, minerals, and the like, such as indigo blue and "turkey" red, which is made from the root of the madder plant, commonly found in Anatolia. The hue, strength, and colorfastness of natural dyes vary wildly.[29] In addition, some early synthetic dyes, such as Perkin's synthetic purple and claret, were notoriously fugitive, often fading to a brown (see figure 1.3). Such fabrics are therefore particularly susceptible to

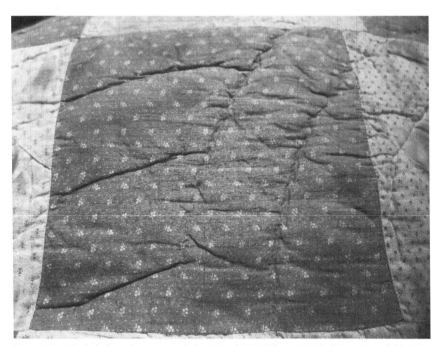

Figure 1.3.   Faded claret dye on a quilt from the 1880s. The original claret color of this print is only apparent in the heavy creases in the fabric. Collection of the author.

light and particularly difficult to exhibit in a museum setting. Natural dark brown dyes, on the other hand, are known for eating away at the fabric completely due to the presence of an iron mordant that was required to produce a really deep, dark brown. Oxidization of the dye over time, or "dye rot," and bleeding of the dye (the inappropriate transmission of the dye to nearby fabric of another color when wet) are two other common preservation concerns of historic textiles. Long-term exposure to light is especially damaging to these sorts of textiles.

Online collections of material culture, such as the Quilt Index, foster the preservation of textiles by putting digital surrogates of the works on permanent display without displaying, and thereby without harming, the physical object. As Stephen Ostrow noted in *Digitizing Historical Pictorial Collections for the Internet*, "Even if a researcher uses digital access for the very restricted purpose of determining which images he wishes to see in the original, the process will contribute greatly to their preservation by reducing their handling and exposure to light."[30] It bears noting that while the primary preservation function of the Quilt Index is the preservation of textile objects and their digital surrogates, the index has branched out to inclusion of quilt-related ephemera, such as awards, patterns, photographs, sketches, and newspaper clippings, and to extended oral histories of quiltmakers in partnership with the Quilt Alliance's Quilters' Save Our Stories[31] project. And, while perhaps less of an issue today given the supposed colorfastness of modern dyes, the rapid digitization of contemporary textile projects creates a reference for future comparisons and analyses of the effects of aging.

Preserving Digital Objects

Many readers will no doubt be familiar with the preservation and conservation of material textile objects, but what about the preservation of their digital surrogates? In her essay titled "Preservation," Abby Smith noted that preservation by benign neglect can work fairly well for paper documents and some kinds of material culture. Great-Grandmother's letters and sewing notions forgotten in the attic in the 1940s, for example, can be found there today in reasonably good condition, assuming there was no water or pest damage. One crazy quilt (see figure 1.4), now in my own collection, spent about seventy-five years in a box, suffering excessive silk shattering; this is certainly not an ideal state of preservation, but the object is still viable. Smith cautions, however, that preservation of digital objects absolutely cannot occur by benign neglect.

Figure 1.4.   Shattering. Collection of the author.

Digital objects create new preservation challenges for museums and archives. One would not, however, expect screenshots I have taken of the Quilt Index and saved to my laptop in the course of researching this chapter to be easily accessible or well preserved for people who happen upon my laptop in the attic seventy years from now. According to Smith, it is ideal for digital objects to be optimized for preservation at the time of their creation.[32] Besides a more active preservation being essential for digital objects, such as my collection of screenshots, digital objects present other preservation challenges as well. Media degradation and the obsolescence of hardware and software significantly challenge the future history of digital material culture. The belief that objects of digital material culture are *permanent*—that is, that they can be preserved and accessed for an almost infinite amount of time to come—is key to the understanding of these objects as material culture in the traditional sense of the word.

Digital Objects beyond Preservation

Digital objects raise questions of not only preservation but also curation and interpretation. All aspects of museum work, from exhibition design and informal learning to conservation and preservation, will need to change as digital objects make their way into collections. In her essay "Redefining Digital Art,"

Beryl Graham describes digital media in the museum as forced into binaries of object for interpretation or object on exhibition. She proposes a taxonomical binary of digital art in museums: either digital objects in museums can be used to interpret traditional, analog objects or they can be exhibited as objects in their own right. According to Graham, "As reflected in this book [*Theorizing Digital Cultural Heritage: A Critical Discourse*], digital interpretation is relatively well researched, has international standards, and benefits from regular expert conferences such as ICHIM and Museums and the Web. The same cannot be said for digital art."[33] While digital objects as interpretive tools have been much studied in the museum technology community, digital objects as works in museum collections have been studied to a lesser extent.

How do these objects fit into the larger history of material culture? Digital objects are often read very differently (as are all objects) depending upon the environment and culture in which they were produced. Jules David Prown and Kenneth Haltman define material culture in their anthology *American Artifacts* as "the manifestation of culture through material productions."[34] They go on to write,

> And the study of material culture is the study of material to understand culture, to discover the beliefs—the values, ideas, attitudes and assumptions—of a particular community or society at a given time. The underlying premise is that human made objects reflect, consciously or unconsciously, directly or indirectly, the beliefs of the individuals who commissioned, fabricated, purchased or used them, and by extension, the beliefs of the larger society to which these individuals belonged.[35]

Based upon Prown and Haltman's definition, one can certainly understand a digital surrogate as material culture. Nowhere do they state that an object must be *real* (in the brick-and-mortar sense of the word) to reflect the values of its maker. "The common perception that digital creations are not permanent is among the chief obstacles to the widespread adoption of digital publishing, and few scholars are rewarded and promoted for their work in this area."[36] Published years ago, this perception is still, regrettably, a popular one among academics. The acknowledgment of the permanence of digital artifacts generally (including online journal articles) is one of the most important mental leaps that scholars will need to make in the early twenty-first century.

Preserving the Textual Record

James Brown famously said that "the one thing that can solve most of our problems is dancing." I would like to amend that statement just a bit. For any digital preservation project, the one thing that can solve most of our problems is . . . a quality metadata scheme. I say this because the information about a material object that gets preserved is largely determined by the metadata scheme adopted for the objects in that collection. This is the controlled vocabulary that calls for the description of everything from the object's title, maker, provenance location, and date to copyright information.

There are many standard vocabularies for metadata out there, from Dublin Core[37] to VRA Core[38] to unique vocabularies specific to the collection, often authored in-house. Though it can create problems down the line in terms of interoperability of databases with other collections and institutions, I tend to favor the latter approach for textile collections. According to Melissa Terras, author of *Digital Images for the Information Professional*, "It is clear that those wishing to describe image data have a wealth of choices to make regarding which metadata schemas to use when describing image resources, but the choice of metadata schema itself should also be made in tandem with choosing the most appropriate structured vocabulary for the objects in question."[39] Textile objects have many rich details that cannot be described by a standardized scheme like Dublin Core. The metadata scheme created for the Quilt Index by index staff, in consultation with other experts in the field, reveals the power, flexibility, and relative ease of custom vocabularies for describing textile objects such as quilts.

The Quilt Index Comprehensive Fields

The Quilt Index Comprehensive Fields[40] is a massive metadata scheme with over 150 unique fields for data entry. The basic, or "core," fields are as follows:

1. Administrative fields
    - Contributing institution's collection or project name
    - Contributing institutional inventory control numbers
    - Alternative inventory control number
2. Descriptive fields
3. Quilt description fields
    A. Overall quilt description
        - Type of quilt object
        - Quilt's title
        - Owner's name for quilt's pattern
        - Alternate name(s) for quilt's pattern in common use
        - Brackman number
        - Overall width measurement (specify unit of measure)
        - Overall length measurement (specify unit of measure)
        - Predominant color(s)

- Quilt-specific colors
- Comments or notes on quilt's condition or repair history
- Content of inscription(s)
- Time period
- Date quilt begun
- Date quilt finished
- Family/owner's date for quilt
- Other date estimation by whom
- Further information concerning date(s)

B. Quilt top description
- Layout format
- Subject of quilt

C. Quilt top materials and construction
- Fabric fiber types
- Fabric types
- Fabric patterns, styles, motifs, or print categories
- Other fiber, fabric, or fabric print types
- Piecing
- Appliqué
- Novelty
- Embellishment
- Unique or other construction
- Embellishment materials used in top

D. Quilt back materials and construction
- Fabric fiber types

E. Quilting description
- Quilting techniques

F. Quilt notes and observations
- Any other features or notes about the quilt's appearance, materials, or construction

G. Quiltmaker identification
- If quilting group, group name
- Quilt top made by
- Quilted by
- Other people who worked on this quilt

H. Quilt provenance
- City
- County
- Reservation
- State

- Province
- Country
- Occasion, date, person inherited from, etc.
- Any additional stories or notes about the quilt's ownership or history

   I. Quilt purpose/uses
- Quilt was originally designed to be used as

   J. Quilt design and materials sources
- Any additional notes or stories about the quilt's design or materials source

  K. Quilt ownership and contact information
- Public/private ownership
- Name of quilt owner

  4. Quiltmaker fields (people)
- Notes or stories about the quiltmaker
- Available sources for quiltmaker

  5. Image fields
- Institutional accession/inventory numbers of image
- Photo credit
- Access and copyright information for image
- For holder of copyright, contact
- Credit line/surveyed by
- For copy restriction, contact
- Data verification[41]

A thorough perusal of just this shortened list yields several fields that are quilt or textile specific, such as Brackman number; quilt-specific colors; fabric patterns, styles, motifs, or print categories; fabric fiber types; piecing; appliqué; embellishment; and quilting techniques. A few examples of the controlled vocabularies within these fields show just how descriptive and textile focused a custom scheme can be. For example, the field on embellishment gives those doing the data entry the following options:

Field 39 (EmbMatF039): Embellishment materials used in top:
  CHECK BOX
Relates to quilt's age, intended purpose, quilter's reason for making the quilt

- Beads attached
- Buttons attached
- Charms attached

- Chenille thread
- Cotton thread
- Metallic thread
- Ribbon thread
- Silk thread
- Synthetic thread
- Wool thread
- Can't tell
- Other attachments
- Other[42]

And the field on so-called quilt-specific colors reads:

Field 14a (QuiltSpecColorF014a): Quilt-specific colors: check all that
apply. CHECK BOX
Very specific "quilty" colors that often reveal specific fabrics,
historical time period, or quilting methods. Those used
interchangeably are listed on the same line separated by "or."

- Bubblegum Pink
- Butterscotch
- Cadet Blue
- Cheddar Orange or Antimony or Chrome Orange
- Chocolate Brown or Hershey Brown
- Chrome Green
- Chrome Yellow
- Claret or Wine
- Double Pink
- Indigo Blue
- Lancaster Blue
- Madder Brown
- Madder Orange
- Madder Red or Cinnamon Red
- Manganese Bronze
- Nile Green
- Prussian Blue or Lafayette Blue
- Turkey Red[43]

"However, it may be the case that these tools [such as Dublin Core] do
not correspond to an individual collection, and metadata creators will de-
cide that the most appropriate approach is to create their own structured

vocabulary which suits and reflects the contents of their individual collection."[44] Without such custom, controlled vocabulary fields, this data about the object would likely never be preserved.

As we will see in chapter 2, custom metadata fields also promote a richer experience in searching the database for objects, and thus, improved access. It is important to note, however, that in choosing to use a custom scheme rather than a standard one, with some extra work, interoperability can still be accomplished. At the Quilt Index, for example, there is a separate, much shorter metadata scheme that is based on the Comprehensive Fields and Dublin Core compliant. In the world of metadata, one can thoroughly describe their cake and share it with others, too.

Of course, the sheer volume of data that such a rich, custom metadata scheme allows for can be a bit off-putting to the casual user. The Quilt Index circumvents this problem by displaying a "brief" version of the record one click in, and offering an option to see the full record with another click. An example of a brief Quilt Index record reads:

> Quilt Title: *Vanne Pique Fest Onee Rouge* [see figure 1.5]
> Pattern Names: French Quilt
> Period: 1876–1900
> Location Made: France
> Project Name: Michigan State University Museum Collection
> Contributor: Michigan State University Museum
> ID Number: 11.0034

Figure 1.5.   Basic Quilt Index record for *Vanne Pique Fest Onee Rouge*. Courtesy of the Quilt Index and the Michigan State University Museum.

Layout Format: Wholecloth
Quilt Size: 59" x 59"
Fabrics: Cotton
Colors: Brown
Quilting Techniques: Hand quilting
Detail Images: No additional images uploaded

These brief records are simply for the sake of usability, though, and not for preservation.

In terms of preservation, it is the full record for the quilt that provides additional information about the quilt's condition: fair/worn (field Over-CondF015) and with fading, tears or holes, and wear to edge or binding (field DamageF016). Field DesignF052d, a text-entry field rather than a controlled vocabulary list in a pull-down menu, describes the quilt's design: "Quilted in the center is a medallion with the initials EB. Surrounding the center is a double line hanging diamond grid. Then triple line quilting into a border of feathered vine on a single line 1/4" diagonal quilting. Then 4 lines of straight quilting into outline quilting in the scallops. The quilting is about 1/4" apart."[45]

Content Management and Metadata Schemes

There are many content management systems on the market today, such as PastPerfect and Argus, designed for collections of objects. Many digital preservation and access projects choose to build their own using open source software. This allows for greater customization and control in-house. Omeka is, as of 2015, the most popular of the open source platforms for preserving and sharing collections. The Quilt Index, however, is housed in a platform called KORA, which was designed at Michigan State University specifically for use with the index. For standardization and interoperability, both Omeka and KORA can be matched with Dublin Core.

I worked with KORA and the Quilt Index Comprehensive Fields for several years, as well as coauthored a metadata scheme for describing American Indian and Native Hawaiian baskets. My advice to anyone creating a custom metadata scheme for a textile collection is (1) be specific and don't be afraid of minutia, (2) think carefully about which fields should have a controlled vocabulary list and which should allow for freestyle entry of text, (3) think about the various aspects of the object type—whether it is a quilt, embroidery, costume, and so on—that make it unique, but also remember to (4) focus on the physical object *and* its maker and their story, (5) consult with other experts on the type of object, and (6) think in terms of preservation *and* access—what information about the object should be preserved with its digital surrogate and what information about the object will most facilitate searches of the collection's database.

Paper Records and Preservation

While all of this undoubtedly seems quite technical and quite, well, digital, it bears noting that the raw data that is being digitized here still largely comes from paper records. Earlier in this chapter, I mentioned that many of the quilt documentation projects were completed in the 1980s. In the past several years, many of these projects have actually started again,[46] often because they want to revise their cut-off date and preserve more recent quilts. And, largely, they have resumed using the paper forms that were initially created for this purpose back in the 1980s.

An old friend from college messaged me out of the blue the other day. His mother owns a couple fairly valuable (and potentially historically significant) family quilts that she intended to have documented locally in her state. She was quickly disheartened, however, when the quilt documentation project wanted her to fill out several paper forms by hand, in duplicate. The documentation project staff offered no option to e-mail anything. So he contacted me asking for alternatives, assuming I must know of quilt documentation projects with easy online forms and the ability to upload multiple jpegs. Unfortunately, the scenario that he described is pretty standard—while museums and archives are doing tremendous things with digital records and images of quilts, the world of quilt documentation, almost all of which is done through local, grassroots, volunteer projects, has in many cases not yet caught up with the digital age. Obviously, someone has to digitize this data if it makes it into a repository like the Quilt Index. This is where volunteer-driven hand entry of metadata comes in.

Metadata Entry and Database Crosswalks

Since many quilt documentation projects were done using paper records, the data from these papers must be hand entered into KORA, on the back end of the Quilt Index website, by volunteers supplied by the documentation project. Training of volunteers for metadata entry almost always requires multiple instructional sessions via video chat, as volunteers generally live in the state of the documentation project in question. Once trained, the data entry interface that they encounter is relatively straightforward. There are only a few types of data entry: prescribed vocabulary—check one; prescribed vocabulary—check all that apply; short text box; and long, essay-length text box. If the documentation project and the index's fields do not match exactly, the volunteer must use their best judgment as to which field or term from the index's scheme to use, which leads us to the use of database crosswalks.

Even when a documentation project has a digital data file, usually in spreadsheet format in Microsoft Excel, getting that data into a database like KORA or Omeka requires some finagling. In the preface of this book, I noted that, as a graduate research assistant at the Quilt Index, "chief among my many tasks was the double-checking of database crosswalks, spreadsheet documents that provided detailed instructions for the automated dump of quilt-related metadata from a museum's database into KORA, the index's content management system." These crosswalks are generated by staff members at the Quilt Index for the programmers performing the data transfer and give detailed instructions that rectify each of the documentation project or museum's metadata fields and the index's. For example, one might say to let [Name of State Project]'s field "Color" equal Quilt Index Comprehensive Field PredomColorsF014. Individual data options must also be rectified via the crosswalk and these must often be changed by hand in the spreadsheet, using the Find and Replace function, *before* the crosswalk is given to the programmers. A documentation project's option of "Cheddar Orange," for example, would need to be rewritten in the spreadsheet as the option appears in Quilt Index field QuiltSpec-ColorF014a, which would be "Cheddar Orange or Antimony or Chrome Orange." Happily, the Replace All function allows a large number of instances of "Cheddar Orange" (say, four hundred) to be replaced all at once.

Now that we have a grasp on the creation of metadata schemes and the entry of metadata, let us turn our attention to the other half of the digital preservation surrogate: the digital image.

Preserving the Digital Image

"Examining a quilt in person is not, of course, the same as viewing quilts online."[47] Because digital images of quilts are, in comparison to the soft and textural physical objects, not entirely satisfying either for the user or from a preservation perspective, digital images of quilts need to be done well. As I will note, though, even a bad digital image is a heck of a lot better than no digital image. But, for now, let us stick to the good ones.

Nuts and Bolts

Key factors to consider in the creation of digital images for preservation are pixels and resolution, compression, and color. As of 2015, a 1600 x 1200 resolution is considered best. The number of pixels per inch, or ppi, depends greatly on the intended use of the image. 72–100ppi is recommended for display on the screen, 300ppi for print access, 400ppi for OCR (optical character recognition), and 600ppi for rare books, manuscripts, and the like.[48] While none of these specifically refer to the preservation of digital surrogates of material objects, erring on the side of quality and choosing 600ppi is a good idea. In terms of compression, there are two types: lossy and lossless. Lossy compression formats (such as .jpg files) discard some of the image data, resulting in a smaller file. Lossless compression (such as .tif files), on the other hand, retains all of the data but results in a much larger digital image file. For access, lossy is just fine because the human eye can fill in the missing data, but for preservation, compression should always be lossless.[49]

As we saw in the section on the preservation of physical textile objects, when it comes to digital preservation of textiles, color is paramount. Preservation images should never be created in grayscale. Instead, 24-bit color (sometimes called "true color" or, on Apple products, "millions of colors") should be used.[50] As Melissa Terras observed,

> Given that colour often imparts much information of importance in cultural and heritage objects and that providing accurate digital images of documents and objects is central to the usefulness of the digitization process, it is obvious that issues of colour and gamma management must be taken seriously by those creating, managing, and delivering data image material in memory institutions.[51]

Human perception of color is impacted by not only absolute, measurable attributes such as brightness, hue, and saturation but also the viewing conditions, the medium of display,[52] and personal preference and culturally constructed meanings.

IT8 is one of the most common International Organization for Standardization (ISO) color management standards. It is "a reflective standard reference consisting of colour bars and greyscales which contain a number of uniform colour patches, to be photographed under the same environmental conditions as the item being captured."[53] Many quilts in the Quilt Index, including the quilts in the Michigan State University Museum Collection, were photographed with a color bar per this standard.

A preservation program for the digital image should include (1) optimization for preservation at the time of creation, (2) the storage of two preservation copies on different servers at different sites, and (3) migration to new formats as the best standards and practices for digital preservation change and evolve. Of course, this ongoing process of creation and optimization, storage, and migration is time consuming and expensive. Sustainability is a huge problem for museum and archival digitization projects because projects are often only funded for a period of just two or three years (and often on a shoestring budget), after which the financial burden of preservation is placed on the institution. Digital collections such as the Quilt Index are almost constantly engaged in the search for funding for long-term preservation. If an institution can manage it, an endowment can be vital in the preservation of such collections.

In preservation, as in all things however, rules are made to be broken. Rather than insisting that all projects submitting quilt data conform to the best standards and practices (though they certainly encourage this), the index casts the widest possible net for preservation. In other words, the Quilt Index does not exclude "bad" photography. Photographs with low resolution, strange artifacts, poor scanning from Kodak slides, no color bars, and so on are better than no photographs at all.

On Photography
While photography was invented in the 1830s,[54] its influence on quilts and quiltmaking came much later than did that of the sewing machine, which as we saw, was made available to the American public by Isaac Singer in the 1850s. Though documentary photography and "art" photography both have their origins in the nineteenth century, it was in the twentieth century that photography really shaped quiltmaking. Documentary photography preserves and disseminates images of quilts and their makers, in contrast to art photography, which tends to fictionalize the visual world; documentary photography seeks simply to document the subject as it presents itself.[55] Cultural documentary photography projects such as the Farm Security Administration's photographs of rural life during the Great Depression or the American Folklife Center's *Blue Ridge Harvest: A Regions Folklife in Photographs* captured and preserved visual data about quilts, quiltmakers, and communities that would otherwise have been lost. Beginning in the early 1980s as part of a movement of regional documentation projects, photography has become one of the most important research tools for quilt historians. State, regional, and local quilt documentation projects take at least one archival photograph of each quilt documented to preserve the visual data for researchers. Quilts themselves are large, cumbersome, and easily damaged. Often it is more practical to do research using photographs of the objects rather than use the quilts themselves.

Photography also permits for the dissemination of quilt designs and quilt research through books, magazines, the Web, and exhibition catalogs. Photographic evidence of quilts exists in newspapers from the colonial revival period and even earlier. While documentary photographs are often created for dissemination in books and online media rather than through exhibition in galleries, the power of documentary photography is nonetheless immense. In *On Photography* (1977), Susan Sontag described the power of the photographic document thus:

> Between two fantasy alternatives, that Holbein the Younger had lived long enough to have painted Shakespeare or that a prototype of the camera had been invented early enough to have photographed him, most Bardolators would choose the photograph. This is not just because it would presumably show what Shakespeare really looked like, for even if the hypothetical photograph were faded, barely legible, a brownish shadow, we would probably still prefer it to another glorious Holbein. Having a photograph of Shakespeare would be like having a nail from the True Cross.[56]

What Sontag is describing about documentary photography relates to Walter Benjamin's idea of the *aura* of the work of art, a concept to which we will return shortly.

Photography has also allowed quiltmakers to become familiar with the stunning diversity of quilts and quilt designs made around the world. The dissemination of photographic images of works particularly highly regarded by scholars and critics has also allowed for the creation of an emerging canon of "great works" in various media, including painting and quilts. The first book to reach a mass audience with quilt images was Safford and Bishop's *America's Quilts and Coverlets* (1972). The photographs of the quilts in the catalog of pioneering quilt history scholar Cuesta Benberry and Joyce Gross's exhibition, *20th Century Quilters: Women Make Their Mark*, have reached infinitely more quiltmakers and scholars than did the actual quilts themselves. Cyril Nelson's quilt engagement calendars, which also predated the Internet, did much to disseminate photographic images of quilts to a large audience and create a popular canon of quilt images.

The Quilt in the Age of Digital Reproduction

What becomes of the aura of the quilt in the age of digital reproduction? This is a problem that has interested me for some time. Indeed, a major result of the multiplicity of online quilt images in the age of digital reproduction is a fundamental shift in what Walter Benjamin called the *aura* of the work of art, that "the work of art [in this case, the quilt] reproduced becomes the work of art designed for reproducibility."[57] In his 1935 essay "The Work of Art in the Age of Mechanical Reproduction," Walter Benjamin theorized on what the photograph and the multiplicity of images have done to the original object, a line of inquiry that has only become more salient today. "Technical reproduction," he wrote, "can put the copy of the original into situations which would be out of reach for the original itself. Above all, it enables the original to meet the beholder halfway, be it in the form of a photograph or a phonograph record. The cathedral leaves it locale to be received in the studio of a lover of art; the choral production, performed in an auditorium or in the open air, resounds in the drawing room."[58] Through photography and its dissemination in print and online, the quilt leaves the exhibition, museum, or the private home of a stranger, to be viewed by the quiltmaker, student, or scholar, in their home, office, or, thanks to smartphones and other mobile devices, anywhere in the world. Furthermore, according to Benjamin, photography and its dissemination has not only altered the ways in which people consume quilts and other works of art but also fundamentally changed the nature of the creative process, as well as the nature of the works of art themselves.

It is necessary to back up a bit before proceeding, however, and say a few words about the work of art before the age of mechanical, photographic, or digital reproduction—about the work of art in the age of handmade reproduction. Benjamin noted early on in his essay that reproductions of works of art were not a new phenomenon, even in the nineteenth century.

> In principle a work of art has always been reproducible. Man-made artefacts could always be imitated by men. Replicas were made by pupils in the practice of their craft, by masters for diffusing their works, and, finally, by third parties in the pursuit of gain. Mechanical reproduction of a work of art, however, represents something new. Historically, it advanced intermittently and in leaps at long intervals, but with accelerated intensity. The Greeks knew of only two procedures for technically reproducing works of art: founding and stamping. Bronzes, terracottas, and coins were the only art works which they could produce in quantity. All others were unique and could not be mechanically reproduced. With the woodcut graphic art became mechanically reproducible for the first time, long before script became reproducible by print.[59]

Photography, most obviously, transformed the artistic process by allowing for the quick and veracious reproduction of works of art, as well as scenes from the world in which we live. "For the first time in the process of pictorial reproduction, photography freed the hand of the most important artistic functions which henceforth devolved only upon the eye looking into a lens."[60] Besides changing the ways in which art and reproductions of works of art are made, reproductions and multiples have also changed the context in which works of art are understood, the exhibition value of quilts and other art works, and transformed the significance of works of art from a ritual to a political value. Photography and the mechanical and digital reproduction of images render the work of art atemporal, which can mean that the context of the viewer is radically different from the context in which the work was originally created. As with the previous example of handmade replicas of Greek statuary, this is not necessarily a new phenomenon. "An ancient statue of Venus, for example, stood in a different traditional context with the Greeks, who made it an object of veneration, than with the clerics of the Middle Ages, who viewed it as an ominous idol."[61] What mechanical and now digital reproduction has done, however, is dramatically quicken the pace at which images of works of art created across all geographies and moments in time are consumed.

The dissemination of reproductions of photographic images precipitated the exhibition value of works of art. Artistic works no longer needed to be created to serve a religious, political, or domestic function. Instead, a new social function—simply to be seen—emerged. This led to the idea of "art for art's sake" among late nineteenth-century artists working in a broad range of disciplines: *L'art pour l'art*, or, more specifically for our purposes, *Le quilt pour le quilt*. Quilts created for exhibition or artistic expression often lack what Benjamin calls the ritual value of historic and traditional quilts. Rather than being made as a warm bedcovering or for a trousseau, such quilts are, more consciously, made to be seen. "With the different methods of technical reproduction of a work of art, its fitness for exhibition increased to such an extent that the quantitative shift between the two poles [cult value and exhibition value] turned into a qualitative transformation of its nature."[62] Essentially, Benjamin's reference to the change in use and meaning of photographs can be applied to the change in use and meaning of quilts.

The essential principle of the individual work of art, the work's sense of gravitas, and that which connects the viewer to the maker (at least to the modern Western notion of the maker) is what Benjamin called the *aura* of a work of art. This aura was both destroyed and created by the ways in which people consumed and understood mechanical photographic reproductions—destroyed because the reproduction breaks the physical connection with the maker, and created because the idea of the veneration of the presence of the maker within the work of art was inconceivable in the time before mechanical reproduction, before artist and art work were estranged from each other by photography. Indeed, for Benjamin, "The presence of the original is the prerequisite to the concept of authenticity."[63] Thus, reproductions and multiples, through photographs, actually *add* to the aura of quilts and other works of art.

What exactly *is* the aura of the quilt, specifically, as opposed to that of, say, the painting? Beyond the definition of aura put forward by Benjamin for works of fine art such as paintings and statuary, the concept of the quilt's aura must also take into account the ways in which the quiltmaker often diverges from the modern notion of the artist, as well as the qualities of warmth and belonging traditionally associated with quilts, what Benjamin would call the quilt's ritual function.[64] The aura of the quilt is thus most commonly an aura of softness and comfort, motherhood and sisterhood, tradition and community, adhering to the perceived and accepted boundaries of form and function. Such an aura is already quite at odds with that of the modern painting, which can often be said to carry an aura of genius and individualism, sometimes even angst or madness, and a breaking of expectations of form and function.

If the aura of the quilt is at odds with that of the modern painting, it seems at first that the aura of the quilt might be even less at home when conveyed through a digital photographic reproduction. How does this already complicated concept of the quilt's aura relate to digital photographic reproductions of quilts, such as those on the Quilt Index? A digital image in an online repository demonstrates the power of the photographic document and, as Benjamin would have argued, raises the exhibition value of quilts, both photographic copies and original objects. Put another way, the Quilt Index and its digital reproductions have enhanced the aura of American quilts.

Some of the quilts that could be said to be the richest in aura are the panels of the NAMES Project's AIDS Memorial Quilt (see figure 1.6).[65]

Figure 1.6.   AIDS Memorial Quilt, NAMES Project. Photo by Elvert Barnes.

Currently, only individual panels uploaded through state documentations exist on the Quilt Index, but a digitization project is on the horizon. These quilt panels carry a tremendous aura individually and collectively for many reasons: because of its sheer scale (weighing over 50 tons, it is the largest piece of folk art in the world), because each 3 x 6 foot panel represents a life lost prematurely to AIDS, and because of the bigotry and cruelty that the sick faced in the 1980s and 1990s (and sometimes still face today). While viewing the quilt online is not as moving as viewing the original object in person, the fact that there are massively multiple images of the quilt serves to heighten the power and mystique of the original.

Much of the body of quilt data on the Quilt Index refers to quilts in common patterns made by ordinary people whose names might have otherwise been lost to history or by anonymous makers. These quilts might largely be called "traditional" quilts. When experiencing these traditional quilts in person, the aura largely lies in the perception on the part of the viewer of the warmth and comfort—as well as historical, cultural, and social issues—that the quiltmaker might have imbued in the object. What becomes of this aura of the warmth and comfort of the solicitous quiltmaker in the age of not only multiple photographic reproductions of the quilt but also thousands of digital reproductions of quilts housed in a database? Does the vast number of digital copies cancel out the warm and handmade qualities of the originals in the viewer's mind, or, as with the previous examples, does this enormous body of digital multiples actually enhance—perhaps even create—the aura of the American quilt?

The Digital Image

Writing in 1843, four years after the invention of the camera, Ludwig Feuerbach wrote in the preface to the second edition of *The Essence of Christianity* that "our era prefers the image to the thing, the copy to the original, the representation to the reality, appearance to being."[66] This seems quite prescient given the proliferation of digital images in the early twenty-first century and their use in many facets of daily life, from entertainment to scholarship. Today, this fascination with digital images is so pervasive that contemporary textile designer Dion Yang titled one of her characteristically quirky fabric designs *Digital Image*. The motifs were hand drawn but digitally printed onto silk chiffon.[67] The use of a digital technique for printing a complicated multicolor pattern on silk decidedly recalls Jacquard's use of punch cards to print a complex rose pattern on silk brocade two centuries earlier.

Representations of objects can be as compelling as the objects themselves. Indeed, in the early twenty-first century, we have come to fetishize the digital image perhaps even *more* than the original object. As Susan Sontag wryly noted in *On Photography*, "Photography is the reality; the real object is often experienced as a letdown."[68] While we might not yet prefer the digital quilt image to the original textile, the digital images (and textual records) of quilts and other textiles are essential in fostering the long-term preservation of the physical object. As we will see in the chapter 2, these images and records also foster an unprecedented level of public access to textile collections.

Notes

1. The Quilt Index is a joint project of The Alliance for American Quilts, MATRIX: Center for Humane Arts, Letters and Social Sciences Online at Michigan State University, and the Michigan State University Museum. The project has been supported in part by major grants from the National Endowment for the Humanities and the Institute for Museum and Library Services, along with the Susan Salser Family Foundation.

2. As of 2015, the Quilt Index holds images and metadata for over sixty thousand quilts and quilted objects. This number is always growing, however, and the index is poised to reach one hundred thousand objects soon.

3. See Marsha MacDowell et al., "Quilted Together: Material Culture Pedagogy and the Quilt Index, a Digital Repository of Thematic Collections," *Winterthur Portfolio* 47, no. 2/3 (2011): 144–45, for a history of the development of the Quilt Index.

4. MacDowell et al., "Quilted Together," 145.

5. Barbara Brackman, *Patterns of Progress: Quilts in the Machine Age* (Los Angeles: Autry Museum of Western Heritage, 1997), 10–11.

6. Julie Wosk, *Women and the Machine: Representations from the Spinning Wheel to the Electronic Age* (Baltimore: Johns Hopkins University Press, 2001), 31.

7. Brackman, 23.

8. Brackman, 23.

9. Judy Heim and Gloria Hansen, *The Quilter's Computer Companion* (San Francisco: No Starch Press, 1998), 53.

10. Heim and Hansen, 54.

11. Love Jonsson, "Rethinking Dichotomies: Crafts and the Digital," in *NeoCraft: Modernity and the Crafts*, ed. Sandra Alfoldy (Halifax: Press of the Nova Scotia College of Art and Design, 2007), 247.

12. Elizabeth Cumming, "Pure Magic: The Power of Tradition in Scottish Arts and Crafts," in *NeoCraft: Modernity and the Crafts*, ed. Sandra Alfoldy (Halifax: Press of the Nova Scotia College of Art and Design, 2007), 173.

13. Charles Eastlake, *Hints on Household Taste*, reprint (New York: Dover, 1986), 199.

14. Eileen Jahnke Trestain, *Dating Fabrics: A Color Guide* (Paducah, KY: American Quilter's Society, 1998), 93.

15. Turkey (named for the country, not the poultry) red refers a red dye made from the roots of the madder plant. Popular throughout the nineteenth century, turkey red was highly sought after because of its colorfastness.

16. The department store was still a very new phenomenon in the 1870s. Its predecessor, the dry goods store (which flourished into the twentieth century in rural areas), had been developed in the 1830s as the old guild system was dying out. Dry goods stores used advertising and competitive pricing to entice customers, a practice that the guild system had not allowed to flourish. The most obvious trend in material culture that aided the rise of the department store was the development of ready-made clothing. Whereas before stores sold fabrics, a totally new type of textile product, off-the-rack apparel, allowed for new types of shopping to emerge.

17. Laurel Thatcher Ulrich, *The Age of Homespun: Objects and Stories in the Creation of an American Myth* (New York: Alfred A. Knopf, 2001), 17.

18. Trestain, 68.

19. Trestain notes that at the end of that very issue of *Lady's Friend* are advertisements for Grovers and Bakers sewing machines, each for the price of $55.

20. The Seamsters Union (Local #500), *The Sun Sets on Sunbonnet Sue*, ca. 1979, from Michigan State University Museum, Michigan State University Museum Collection. Published in the Quilt Index, http://www.quiltindex.org/basicdisplay.php?kid=1E-3D-1.

21. The quilt is pictured in figure 1.2, the screenshot of the Quilt Index main page.

22. Given at the *Recent Advances in Conservation* conference, Rome, 1961.

23. Agnes Geijer, "Preservation of Textile Objects," in *Changing Views of Textile Conservation*, eds. Mary M. Brooks and Dinah D. Eastop (Los Angeles: Getty Conservation Institute, 2011), 79.

24. Luke Haynes, *But I Know Crazy* (Second place, Ages 30 and Under), 2009, from Quilt Alliance, Crazy for Quilts. Published in the Quilt Index, http://www.quiltindex.org/basicdisplay.php?kid=1–6–9F.

25. For the Signature Quilt Project, see http://www.quiltindex.org/sqpgalleries.php.

26. Kathryn L. Hatch, *Textile Science* (Minneapolis-Saint Paul: West Publishing, 1993), 57–67.

27. Geijer, 79–80.

28. Hatch, 427.

29. Hatch, 432.

30. Stephen Ostrow, *Digitizing Historical Pictorial Collections for the Internet* (Washington, DC: Council on Library and Information Resources, 1998), 9.

31. For Quilters' Save Our Stories, see http://www.allianceforamericanquilts.org/qsos/.

32. Abby Smith, "Preservation," in *A Companion to Digital Humanities*, eds. Susan Schreibman et al. (Oxford: Blackwell, 2004), 583.

33. Beryl Graham, "Redefining Digital Art," in *Theorizing Digital Cultural Heritage*, eds. Fiona Cameron and Sarah Kenderdine (Cambridge, MA: MIT Press, 2007), 94.

34. Jules David Prown and Kenneth Haltman, eds., *American Artifacts: Essays in Material Culture* (East Lansing: Michigan State University Press, 2000), 11.

35. Prown and Haltman, 11.

36. Smith, 576.

37. See Dublin Core Metadata Initiative, http://dublincore.org.

38. See VRA Core, http://core.vraweb.org.

39. Melissa Terras, *Digital Images for the Information Professional* (London: Ashgate, 2008), 179.

40. The fields were developed by Quilt Index staff in conjunction with the Michigan State University Museum and the Michigan Quilt Project, the Illinois State Museum and the Illinois Quilt Research Project, the Tennessee State Library and Archives and Quilts of Tennessee, and the University of Louisville Records and Archives and the Kentucky Quilt Project.

41. MacDowell et al., 155–56.

42. Quilt Index Comprehensive Fields, February 16, 2009, revision.

43. Quilt Index Comprehensive Fields.

44. Terras, 179.

45. *Vanne Pique Fest Onee Rouge* (maker not recorded), 1876–1900, from Michigan State University Museum, Michigan State University Museum Collection. Published in the Quilt Index, http://www.quiltindex.org/fulldisplay.php?kid=1E-3D-2614.

46. The Quilt Index Wiki maintains a list of the quilt documentation projects, including when they were held, how many quilts were documented, whether the projects' files have been added to the Quilt Index, and any other pertinent information about the project. See http://www.quiltindex.org/wiki/index.php/United_States.

47. MacDowell et al., 145.

48. Terras, 41–43.

49. Terras, 51–42.

50. Terras, 47.

51. Terras, 187.

52. Terras, 186.

53. Terras, 189.

54. The first fixed photographic image that did not fade was created in 1839 by Louis Daguerre, almost exactly a century before Walter Benjamin wrote "The Work of Art in the Age of Mechanical Reproduction."

55. In *Documentary Expression and Thirties America*, William Stott defines the documentary in photography in two ways, as the presentation of fact, and as the "human documentary," which visually presents human emotions about real life events. For the purposes of this discussion, I use *documentary* in the former sense.

56. Susan Sontag, *On Photography* (New York: Farrar, Straus and Giroux, 1977), 154.

57. Walter Benjamin, "The Work of Art in the Age of Mechanical Reproduction," in *Commerce and Culture: From Pre-Industrial Art to Post-Industrial Value*, ed. Stephen Bayley (Tunbridge Wells, Kent: Penshurst Press, 1989), 36.

58. Benjamin, 36.

59. Benjamin, 35.

60. Benjamin, 35.

61. Benjamin, 36.

62. Benjamin, 37.

63. Benjamin, 35.

64. Benjamin, 36.

65. NAMES Project Foundation, http://www.aidsquilt.org/about/the-names -project-foundation.

66. Quoted in Sontag, 153.

67. Drusilla Cole, *Textiles Now* (London: Lawrence King, 2008), 103.

68. Sontag, 147.

Access

I N AN ARTICLE IN THE *WALL STREET JOURNAL* TITLED "Still Life With Badly Dressed Museum-Goer," journalist, humorist, and cultural critic Joe Queenan asked, "People go to museums to see beautiful things: madonnas, knights in white satin, glorious sunsets, improbably muscular stallions, anything that's classy. Why, then, do they dress like pigs?"[1] The essay is a satirical take on visitors' sartorial faux pas; for example, Queenan positively states, "People in deliberately torn, tattered clothes should only get to see visions of hell by Hieronymus Bosch."[2] But behind the satire lies a truth. Many people who would dress up for a nice dinner out or for the ballet or the opera often look like they got lost on their way to Wally World when they visit a museum. Online, however, we visit museums in our pajamas, luxuriating in comfort and convenience. But, just as supposedly "proper" dress and the barriers to it (from laziness to genuinely poor taste to class and racial prejudice toward certain forms of dress) can limit access to museums in the brick-and-mortar world, there are barriers to museum access in the online world. Some of these are the result of deep-seated social issues (again, race and class) not easily solved by digital technologies that would be more effectively addressed by policy changes at the local, state, and national levels. Other barriers to online access to collections *can* be eradicated, or at least mitigated, with the aid of digital technologies, however, and it is to these that we turn our attention in this chapter.

We love digital collections, and we've come to demand better and better access to them. Online access to collections provides access to those who could not otherwise attend, such as people who live in remote or rural areas, those with certain physical disabilities or chronic illnesses, and students and researchers who previously had to travel to visit multiple physical sites. Online access to images and information has also led to a more democratic display of collections not limited by the physical space of the gallery. In art museums, for example, collections of such objects as textiles and furniture, which are seldom displayed due to lack of space and the primacy of painting, are readily available online.

Museological issues surrounding digital technology existed before the problem of the display, interpretation, and preservation of digital objects, however. For more than a decade, the Web had already been playing a role in a shift in the display of analog textile objects. As W. Logan Fry noted, in the pre-Internet era, museums, working within the spatial constraints of the museum building, focused of the exhibition of the so-called fine arts such as painting and sculpture. The virtual exhibition space afforded by museum websites allowed, for the first time for many museums, the exhibition of their textile collections, including the works of contemporary fabric artists.

> Historically, museums have buried their textile collections in storage vaults, with only a few select pieces from antiquity on display. One obvious reason is that space is at a premium, and museums need to show their Rembrandts and van Goghs. The digital revolution is changing all of this. . . . Once a museum learns how to puts its Manets online, very little effort is needed to add its textile collection as well, including the work of contemporary textile artists.[3]

Thus, the way in which museums used the Web to put collections online not only provided crucial public access to these collections—sometimes for the first time—but also served to elevate the place of the museum textile collection.

What do we mean by "access"? Quite simply, access provides opportunities for the online visitor. In his essay "The Virtual Visit," Roland Jackson described three distinct levels of access to online exhibitions and collections. First is access to data and information. This is the lowest barrier to entry and the least threatening to technophobes. Second is an intermediate level, access to discussion, and third is access to collaboration. This deepest level of access caters to an emerging and growing group of online visitors who "want to create new electronic worlds with others and including those who have an interest in shaping presentations of science and technology according to their own views and interests."[4] Unlike preservation, which is primarily focused upon the objects, access first and foremost serves the human element, and the richest forms of access allow people to enhance or expand on the data and information made available to them.

Almost paradoxically, artificial intelligence, or AI, is increasingly used to facilitate this access. A headline in *Smithsonian Magazine* in May 2015 read, "Computers Are Learning about Art Faster than Art Historians."[5] In the article, Marissa Fessenden noted that, "Computers are getting better at some surprisingly human tasks. Machines can now write novels [though they still aren't great—no AI is the next Hemingway . . . yet], read a person's pain in their grimace, hunt for fossils and even teach each other. And now that museums have digitized much of their collections, artificial intelligence has access to the world of fine art."[6] Should we be concerned? Not really. AI is actually a hugely positive development for art (and dress and textile) history. Soon, thanks to pattern-recognition algorithms, museum staff members, scholars, students, artists, and the general public will be able to search online museum collections visually rather than by searching for text. That is a particularly big deal for nonspecialists who do not necessarily know the fancy jargon for the object for which they are looking. Social tagging is another relatively recent technology that fosters access to collections by crowd-sourcing the tags used to search for objects, resulting in search terms that are in some cases simpler and more likely to actually appear in a user's query. While social tagging has been around for a while, a new and exciting development is that algorithms are now in on the act, supplementing tags that humans seem to have overlooked.

Through the course of this chapter, two technologies: social tagging and pattern recognition—focused on providing better searchability and access through language (metadata) and better visual searchability and access, respectively—undergird the discussion, as does the role of women and gender in access. Roland Jackson's model of access provides the roadmap to the chapter, with sections on "Access to Data and Information," "Access to Discussion: Social Tagging," and "Access to Collaboration: Visual Searching and Pattern Recognition." The chapter ends with a discussion of the open data movement and its call for "raw data now!" in a short section on "The Future of Access: Linked Data."

Access to Data and Information

Providing access to data and information is possibly the most obvious task for which museums and archives use digital technologies. One of the simplest but most impactful means by which collections can provide online access to broad publics is by uploading their images to Flickr Commons.[7] This way, users can search across vast numbers of public and private collections rather than searching a single collection or consortium's database. The Commons provides Creative Commons licensing options for uploaded images ranging from "all rights reserved" to "donated to the public domain" and several shades of gray in between, allowing copyright holders to choose from a menu of options including attribution, no-derivatives, share alike, and commercial/ noncommercial to find the licensing option that is right for their institution.[8]

Donating images of one's collection to the public domain is a truly civic-minded gesture that provides unprecedented access to users. Some might fear that such images will be primarily used for merchandising, and thus for private financial gain that in no ways serves the museum or its mission. But consider that images donated to the public domain are also used by academics publishing scholarly manuscripts. In the age of the adjunctification of academia, fewer and fewer scholars can afford to pay permissions for images for academic publications. Consider also the goodwill and free publicity generated by the donation of museum collections images to the public domain. One of the high-profile museums with a large historic dress and textile collection to have taken this step on Flickr Commons is the Los Angeles County Museum of Art (LACMA).[9] Indeed, many of the images used to illustrate this book were donated to the public domain by LACMA.[10]

Finding and Tagging a Reptile (Fabric)

Because large clearinghouses of images like Flickr Commons search across numerous unrelated collections, results for historic textiles are returned from national and university libraries and archives just as often as, if not more often than, from art museums or even dedicated textile collections. In my own research on eighteenth-century silk, the British Library, the National Archives of Scotland, University of Maryland Libraries, and University of Illinois Library are some of the many libraries and archives I have found to have active Flickr Commons accounts relevant for dress and textile scholarship. This reptilian fabric by Scottish aesthetic movement textile designer Christopher Dresser (see figure 2.1) was uploaded by the National Archives UK. As the National Archives deals with many different kinds of collections, including paper documents, photographs, sound and video, and material culture, only basic metadata—title, description, date, and an object number—are given for the fabric:

> Title: Reptilian Fabric
> Description: Patented textile pattern by Christopher Dresser, one of
>   Victorian Britain's leading industrial designers. This design was
>   intended for dress fabric for the African market.
> Date: August 1887
> Our Catalogue Reference: EXT 9/104 (79119)[11]

This conforms to the Dublin Core Metadata Standards discussed in chapter 1.

Figure 2.1.   Christopher Dresser reptilian fabric for the African market, 1887. Collection of the National Archives (UK).

Supplementing this rather bare bones approach to metadata are tags. Tags add to the vocabulary associated with the object and thus improve access by aiding users in their searches. On Flickr Commons, tags are applied by a combination of the contributing institution or individual, other users wishing to help others find the object, and "robots"—helpful algorithms programmed to add tags that should theoretically be useful based on search patterns for similar objects. Tags submitted by humans appear in gray, while tags submitted by the robots appear in white. If there are few or no white tags for an object, the humans have more or less covered their bases as far as tag generation is concerned. For the Christopher Dresser reptile fabric, human-authored tags include the following:

The National Archives (UK)
textiles
snakes
design
Victorian

Board of Trade
Christopher Dresser
colorful
textile
fashion
fabric
1887
reptilian
schlange [snake]
texildruck [*sic*] [textile printing]
dessin [design]
bunt [colorful]
blau [blue]
schwarz [black]
rot [red]
gelb [yellow]
zunge [tongue]
schielen [squint][12]

Clearly a German-speaking user has been hard at work. The robots applied only one tag for this object: print.[13]

What does all of this tell us about how people search for historic textile objects and how to provide better access to those objects? First of all, the robots called the humans out on a rookie omission. People searching for a textile swatch are often primarily looking by print. "Print" should always be a tag, as should more specific prints, such as paisley, polka dot, stripe, plaid, or check, if applicable. Second, tags like "design," "fabric," "textile," and the designer's name are obvious choices, but others are equally important. The tag "snake" caught my eye as a particularly useful one. Many users searching for this object might not be looking for a historic textile swatch at all but instead will just be looking for any objects of visual culture with snakes on them. Or someone might remember having seen the fabric some-where and search for it without knowing the designer's name (Christopher Dresser). For the user looking for one particular piece, a broad search term like "design," "fabric," or "textile" returns far too many results. Indeed, a search of Flickr Commons limited only to those images donated to the public domain returns 178,527 results for "design," 14,404 for "fabric," and 11,914 for "textile." Searching for this reptilian print using any of those commonsense, but also too common, tags would be like trying to find a needle in a haystack. Conversely, however, a user who is just browsing various historic fabric swatches—whether for schoolwork or design inspiration—would be well served using these general tags. The key here is to put oneself in the shoes of a wide variety of users.

One of the best ways to start thinking like a user is to read user-applied tags. In the case of the German-speaking user's tags, the various colors that appear in the fabric were added along with imaginative and lively words that describe the snake: tongue and squint. These are all great additions to the vocabulary surrounding the object because there are conceivably many reasons why users would search for them but not necessarily be searching for the standard textile tags while doing so. As is made obvious by the previous example, the English-speaking world often takes a rather Anglophone-centric approach to tagging, but clearly users who speak other languages are searching for our material. To provide the best possible access, basic keywords should be given in multiple languages. The languages to use depend on the nature of the object. In this case, it makes sense that a German-speaking user would be interested in Dresser's work, as he was awarded a doctorate *in absentia* by the University of Jena in Germany for his work in the rather Victorian field of "Art Botany."[14]

Finally, we can learn just as much from omission as from inclusion. In this case, in spite of the fact that this fabric was created for the African market, neither the humans nor the robots thought to include tags like "Africa" or "colonialism." Both people and the algorithms that people create are inclined to call attention to the so-called winners of history and leave out the darker bits. Indeed, the tag "colonialism" returned just nineteen public domain images on Flickr Commons. (The tag "colonial" returned a much more impressive 38,451 results but is impractical as a search term for this purpose, as many of the results deal with the thirteen American colonies.) Such an unpopular search term as "colonialism" would be outside a robot's notice as a potential tag, but what about the humans'?

Instagram and Access

While many individual users access image and metadata via large clearing-houses of images such as Flickr Commons, social sites such as Instagram and Tumblr (the latter of which is discussed at length in chapter 3) are also popular destinations for access to images and related information. For those institutions with a Pinterest board but not an Instagram feed, as of the writing of this book in late 2015, Instagram has largely replaced Pinterest as the place where people look for images on the social Web. Undoubtedly this, too, will change with time. This underscores the need for at least one person (preferably two or three) on a museum or archive's staff to be a "technology champion," keeping abreast of the latest digital tools and trends. This field changes quickly, especially online.

Instagram has become a major fixture in the world of contemporary fashion, as seen in the online coverage of New York Fashion Week in September 2015.[15] Beyond fostering access to fashion images and commentary, however, this social platform is also a direct line to the market for designers and makers. Selling art on Instagram was the subject of a 2014 article in *Vogue* magazine. In the article "Why the World's Most Talked-About New Art Dealer Is Instagram," Olivia Fleming writes,

> The social media platform is not only launching the career of under-the-radar artists, it is providing the world with an entirely new way to access art. Where artists once had to first get support of the art world elite—critics, galleries and big name collectors, which would eventually lead to museum shows—before reaching the monied masses, today artists use Instagram as their own virtual art gallery, playing both dealer and curator while their fans become critics and collectors, witnessing the creative process in real time.[16]

Importantly, the access to fashion images uploaded by users to Instagram has been recognized as an important means to facilitate scholarly inquiry. "Instagram and Fashion," a lecture given by Colombian fashion writer Vanessa Rosales and FIT Museum curator Ariele Elia in October 2015, demonstrated Instagram as a tool for primary research in fashion studies.[17]

A Museum of Museums on the Web

While uploading images to a large digital clearinghouse such as Flickr Commons or a social site such as Instagram is one of the best ways to provide public access to collections, these sites do have their drawbacks for museums and archives. Such sites do not allow for the use of extensive custom metadata schemes that, as we saw in chapter 1, facilitate both preservation and access of textile collections. They also may not reinforce the museum's brand and draw traffic to the museum's website. Institution-specific and consortium-specific online access projects solve these problems. Unsurprisingly, there are several wonderful access projects out there, notably the Google Art Project.[18] The Google Art Project uses gigapixel photographic technology to provide the best available visual access to works of art held in a growing consortium of museums around the world. Gigapixel simply refers to one billion (10^9) pixels, the equivalent of a thousand times the sharpness and depth of an image taken by a one-megapixel camera. Amit Sood's TED Talk, "Building a Museum of Museums on the Web,"[19] illustrates exactly "what you get for a billion pixels," drilling down deep into Pieter Bruegel the Elder's painting *The Harvesters* (1565) to reveal in the distant background the depiction of a Shrove Tuesday game of goose-pulling.[20]

While the Google Art Project explores all visual art media, not only textiles, there are textiles included, both as a part of larger museum collections and stand-alone collections, such as the collection of the International Quilt Study Center & Museum (IQSC&M).[21] There have also been highly successful access projects dedicated specifically to textiles, including the Quilt Index (the focus of the case study in chapter 1) and the IQSC&M's Quilt Explorer[22] and World Quilts: The American Story.[23] While these sites are quilt-specific, one site, Tapestry, provides access to individual swatches of fabric themselves, making it an ideal project for a variety of interests in dress and textile studies.

Tapestry

Tapestry[24] is a project of the Design Center at Philadelphia University and provides access to their collection of thousands of historic fabric swatches. According to the Tapestry site's About page, "The fabric samples are the most popular and most vulnerable elements contained within the Textile Collection. Requests to visit and study the images of fabric swatches in the Textile Collection range from students to commercial entrepreneurs to general aficionados of design."[25] Providing access to this collection was thus a major challenge on two levels—the objects themselves are quite fragile and lots of different types of visitors want to see them for different purposes. Indeed, even small swatches of fabric can have historical interest. Most people working in or with a museum textile collection know the power of the curatorial process in turning what might seem like ordinary scraps of fabric into meaningful scraps of history. In "Care of Fabrics in the Museum" (1977), Nobuko Kajitani wrote,

> Unlike most other works of art, the majority of fiber-made objects in the museum was not at the time of manufacture deemed "high art." Instead, they were intended to serve utilitarian purposes in clothing, bedding, and furnishing for people of all social levels. They were often used repeatedly until they were in tatters. What seems an insignificant fragment is in fact significant and reflects an intricate background. Although very few come with historical and personal documentation, museum fabrics themselves provide ample opportunity to research knowns and explore unknowns. . . . In the museum, we have the power to change mere rags and tatters into meaningful objects.[26]

The relationship here between preservation and access is critical; digital preservation fosters better access, and digital access fosters better preservation.

A search of Tapestry for a date, 1975, yields records for twenty-one fabrics made in or around that year.[27] The image-forward display of search results is visually stunning, but searching is made difficult through the use of a keyword search box only, instead of multiple searchable fields, and the metadata provided for each fabric swatch is quite basic. A sample record reads:

Collection ID: 1996.116.36
Date of Manufacture: 1975
Motif Category: Floral
Motif: flowers, branches, leaves, buds
Colors: pink, purple, green, brown, black, red, gray
Weave Structure: satin, jacquard[28]

There are several basic types of textile designs, including floral, conversational (realistic objects), traditional (such as paisley and calicoes), textures and weaves, and abstract and geometric.[29] Prints can incorporate multiple categories at the same time, as in this polyester from the 1970s featuring a mix of floral and geometric motifs (see figure 2.2). Currently, effectively searching textile surface designs requires above all knowledge of the appropriate terminology. In the above example

Figure 2.2.   Print combining geometric and floral motifs, 1970s. Collection of the author.

of a rather easy-to-search-for fabric, one need only know the year of manufacture or basic terms like "satin" and "floral" to effectively find this fabric. "Jacquard" is a term that many users of the site might not know, however. Often, when one is unfamiliar with these terms, one's access to collections is necessarily somewhat limited. The following section explores how we remove this barrier to access caused by an unreasonable assumption that the public will understand the technical of a particular discipline.

Access to Discussion: Social Tagging

Devoré (see figure 2.3), colloquially referred to as "burnout technique," is often applied to velvets. Textile conservator Andie Robertson defines devoré as follows: "Generally classed as a textile-finishing technique, the devoré process of textile ornamentation involves burning away single or multiple fibres from a constructed fabric."[30] Manufacturers developed devoré in the middle of the nineteenth century, and the fabric had its heyday in the 1920s and 1930s, subsequently enjoying a resurgence in popularity in the 1980s.[31] Patterns worked in devoré ran the gamut from the complex to the simple, from florals to modern, geometric designs.[32]

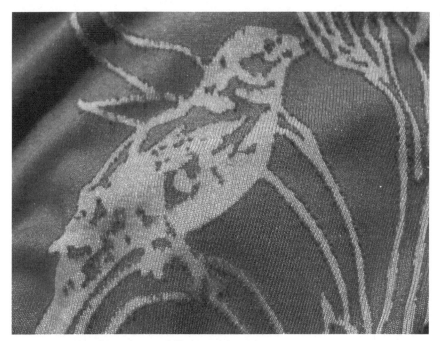

Figure 2.3.   Devoré in polyester. Collection of the author.

Because devoré is not a widely known textile term (even among aca-demics in the field), it is very difficult to provide scholars and the general public access to devoré online. (There are no results found in Tapestry, for example.)

> An additional hindrance to the presence of devoré in textile collections is the problem of distinguishing a devoré textile from a traditionally woven textile. For instance, recognising a cut velvet fabric is often only pos-sible by looking closely at the weave configuration. Analyzing the ragger or fluffy quality of fibre ends is often the only way to determine woven devoré manufacturing. Such expertise and experience is currently all too rare among textile specialists, historians and conservators. The creation of a digital record that would gather together information regarding the design and fabric structure, state of preservation and museum or archive location would perhaps be a start in providing the information that is currently absent from textile scholarship.[33]

As we saw in the last chapter, a good metadata scheme doesn't just foster preservation; it also fosters access. For example, imagine searching a data-base for the fabric-with-designs-burned-out without knowing "devoré," its proper term. What happens when a visit to the collection's website doesn't know the term "devoré"? Here is where social tagging is incred-ibly helpful—and becoming more helpful through the use of AI-applied tags: it could solve the problem of searching for devoré and countless other lesson-known types of textiles.

Social Tagging

As we noted in chapter 1, metadata is data about data. So if the object is the "data," then all the information about the object is the "metadata." For example, let us consider President Abraham Lincoln's top hat. The hat itself is the data. That it is brown-black, from around 1859, made of silk, and known to have been worn at Antietam are all metadata about the object. Let us return to the example of Tapestry and the case of the record for a conversational print manufactured by Black & Co. in Scotland in 1883. The record states that the motifs depicted on the swatch are "coins, currency, and stamps." This is indeed the case, and if one is searching for fabric on the basis that the swatch depicts any of these motifs, then the user is well served by this result. Significantly, the central stamp is one that is highly sought after by philatelists, a one-shilling stamp from the Cape of Good Hope from the 1850s or 1860s. If one searches the Tapestry database for the phrases "South Africa" or "Cape of Good Hope," however, this fabric does not show up in the results. Why? Because museum collections records tend to state the artist or maker, title (and note here that the phrases "South Africa" and "Cape of Good Hope" are not included in the title of this record), provenance location, and accession or collection ID number (this one's is 1996.17.1242), but not the key phrases that might be employed in searching for this fabric.

This problem does not directly impact searches of the database conducted by the staff at the Design Center—their institution owns the object and they likely know its collection ID and other basic metadata if they want to look it up via Tapestry. But for a layperson, maybe a child doing a school report, this is a problem, because they might not know that they're looking for this particular fabric swatch, or, indeed, any fabric at all, but rather just for an illustration of this stamp, the Cape of Good Hope, or African stamps of the nineteenth century. If this Tapestry implemented social tagging of its collections, a process that allows users to add tags (key phrases) to annotate an object's record, someone may very well have tagged this swatch with "Cape of Good Hope," making the painting much easier for folks to find. This is but one example of how providing access to tagging of collections to the general public content is of benefit to both historians and the publics we serve.

Several institutions have already implemented social tagging of their collections, and an early adopter of this technology was the Brooklyn Museum. In their 2009 paper presented at the Museums and the Web conference, Shelley Bernstein and colleagues note, "The goal with tagging on our site is not just to gain search terms, but also to allow our visitors ownership of the collection by tagging on their terms and then attributing those tags publicly to their own accounts."[34] And when they delivered that paper in 2009, users had created over forty-five thousand tags on collection objects and 95 percent of their collection online had been tagged. As Bernstein argues, such tagging not only benefits a museum and its online visitors by improving search terms but also gives users a sense of stakeholdership in the museum enterprise, a sense of being a good citizen and positively contributing to the experience of those who visit the museum's site.

In 2010, the Brooklyn Museum made a mobile version of their *Tag, You're It!* tagging game available, and on the screen you see the process. A user selects an object to tag, in this case a painting by Marsden Hartley, inputs the object's accession number from the bottom left of their screen, tags the object (here the user chose to tag it "dramatic"), and then saves their tag. Hartley's *Painting No. 48* joins 134 other works in the collection searchable as "dramatic" and the user receives five points for adding a tag and four points for having now tagged objects on four different floors of the museum.

Now, you may well be asking yourself at this point, what about people who post tags that are inaccurate or inappropriate or simply irrelevant? While this junk posting does happen from time to time—I myself had to close down edits to the Quilt Index wiki on several occasions because of ads posted for psychic readings, male enhancement, and various prescription drugs—these attacks are by and large made by robots and spider algorithms rather than people, and can be ferreted out with Captchas and other techniques. Actually, in my experience, people who post content online in historical or educational contexts (at least those who post to a quilt history wiki) tend to be very well meaning, intrinsically motivated to share their knowledge and to learn from others. Many of these users are, predictably, women, and it is worthwhile here to step back and explore the changing role of women's access online.

The Wild West

The history of the gendering of access to the World Wide Web is a fascinating one. Moving from the World Wide Web as the Wild West of the 1990s to the Internet as domestic space in the late 2000s, the gender shift online has theoretical implications for our understanding of the intersection of domesticity, motherhood, and Web 2.0 technologies. It is important to remember, however, that the shift from Wild West to domestic space is only one history of gender and the Internet. There are early female adopters with any new technology. The alternate history of the early Web is a history in which either the Wild West is a fallacy or there were at least a few female desperados.

The shift from a wild space primarily dominated by men to a more domestic space primarily inhabited by women, in which even a rural woman in her nineties can be an embodied participant in the digital culture, is indeed one of the many histories of the Internet (and, more specifically, of the World Wide Web). This Wild West did not appear from nowhere. Digital technologies, and even virtual spaces, almost always have a direct analog antecedent not too far back in history. The Web has this history in common with many other technologies, for example, television and radio. Turn-of-the-last-century lantern lectures for the armchair tourist and games of Dungeons and Dragons played out in parents' basements in the late twentieth century, for example, are both examples of analog virtual worlds, direct ancestors of today's virtual worlds and massively multiplayer online games.

In *The American Technological Sublime*, David Nye argued that historically it was only men who were felt to be able to truly experience the sublime. Women had an affinity, not for the awe of the sublime, but rather for the quaintness of the picturesque. In nineteenth-century America, women had an important role to play in the technological sublime, however. Women domesticated once sublime technologies, making men ready to experience and conquer new forms of the sublime. Electricity, once frightening, came to be represented allegorically as a goddess; the roar of the locomotive was somewhat muted when people spoke of the train as feminine ("get on her"); and once monstrous factories were made into mothers, they were said to give birth to the steel. Each of these technologies was feminized over time. The same could be said for twentieth-century technologies such as radio and television. In their earliest stages, these technologies were largely the preserve of men tinkering away in their attics. When made available to consumers for the home, they were positioned at the heart of the living room, encased in wood cabinetry, and used to receive broadcasts of soap operas and the like for the women of the house. While this is certainly a gross oversimplification, there is truth to this narrative to be sure.

Much of the rhetoric surrounding the World Wide Web when it first emerged for the public in the early 1990s was that of a Wild West, a new, lawless world to be conquered and populated by men.[35] Indeed, for at least the first ten years of the Web, pornography was the most visited type of resource on the Internet, not counting e-mail. (Incidentally, pornography, and the desire to consume it in ever more private and easily accessible ways, has been theorized to explain the success of many user-centered technologies. VHS, for example, thrived where the earlier home video format Betamax had failed; VHS caught on in large measure because it allowed people to be titillated in the privacy of their own homes rather than in the movie theater. While there are certainly women who access pornography, it is culturally constructed as a men's pursuit, and this gives further credence to the veracity of the male as early adopter, Wild West history.) Gambling (which conjures up images of saloons in the Old West) was another very popular use in the early days of the Web.

Just as there were women in the Wild West, however (as there were on every new frontier), there were female early adopters of the World Wide Web, and these female early adopters were largely figured as Other. There were websites (news, weather, stupid facts, useful facts, rantings and ravings, etc.), and then there were "women's websites." Of course, the women on the Web used and enjoyed sites featuring news, weather, stupid facts, and the like, but these types of sites would never have been seen as women's sites. Nor, interestingly, would they have been called "men's sites." Normal, plain-old websites were in the 1990s associated with male users, and sites specifically thought of as women's sites were something else, apart from the majority experience of the Web, something Other. In her discussion on websites by sanitary brands in her book *Figures of Fantasy: Internet, Women and Cyberdiscourse*, Susanna Paasonen argues that early websites by brands such as Kotex naively tried to build communities of users based solely on the commonality of menstruation because women were seen as such an isolated and cohesive group on the Web.[36] Kotex .com was not the only imagined haven for women in the Wild West of the World Wide Web. The domestication of the Web began long before social media and other social applications with personal sites that functioned very much as living rooms online. Personal webpages such as "Kathy's Geocities Guinea Pig Appreciation Webring Links Page" provided an outlet for women's (and men's) personal representation and networking from some the earliest days of the Web.

Men outnumbered women in Web 1.0 (though, I would argue, even more so in the public imagination than in actuality), but with Web 2.0 in the early 2000s, women truly claimed the Web as their own. Social sites such as Facebook, Twitter, and Instagram now account for greater Web usage than do pornography sites, and women outnumber men in these social networking Web applications. Women are no longer the Other on the Web. Many of the so-called Web 2.0 sites developed in the first decade of the twenty-first century, such as Shutterfly and Blogher, are targeted to women, and advertising on the Web reflects this. The so-called Mommy Blogger is now one of the most active types online. Women are even becoming a larger percentage of the population in MMORPGs (massively multiplayer online role-playing games) such as *World of Warcraft*.

A far cry from the metaphor of the Wild West used so often to describe the Internet in the 1990s,[37] the Internet has become an increasingly domestic space. "They [craft-related social media] also, as cultural theory acknowledges, establish an ideal—a realm or space, in which shared beliefs relating to an understanding of what knitting [or quilting or weaving] *is*, based on experience and expectation, can be explored and realized."[38] So what, if any, are the implications of a Wild West conquered and domesticated by women? In *Information Please: Culture and Politics in the Age of Digital Machines* (2000), Mark Poster argued that it was the introduction into the home of electronic media that brought down the way of life of the Victorian nuclear family:

> The child's space in the Victorian home lacked all the information technologies we assume today. . . . By the early twenty-first century, the number and variety of information machines installed in the home has increased remarkably. Televisions, answering machines, fax machines, computers, electronic games, network connections, and so many other devices have made entry into the residence. . . . The home has become infinitely permeable to the outside world, with the result that the coherence of the culture of the nuclear family has been fragmented into what I call the segmented family. Each member of the family now sustains a separate cultural world within the family.[39]

Electronic media made the home much more permeable to the outside world and segmented the family, as each member of the family group was allowed to pursue their own interests. As a stereotypical example, a mother could listen to a soap opera, the children to Tom Mix, and the father to the news, without coming back together as a family. This brief sketch of the introduction of radio into the home certainly has parallels to technology usage in the home in the present day, but Poster's model of media and the collapse of the family does not truly fit with the reality of what women are doing in online social networks and photosharing sites. What could be read from the standpoint of "family values" as most sinister in my theoretical example above is the fact that the mother may very well listen to her soap opera lost in reverie, unconcerned for her family, daydreaming of something rather different from her situation in life.

While the Web certainly does allow women to step out of their roles in real life for a time and try on different roles, even different genders in virtual worlds and many online games, much of the work done by women in social networking sites, the very core of what it is to be a Mommy Blogger, is sharing the experience of childrearing and family life with her friends and family. My husband's cousin sends me links to pictures on Shutterfly of her daughter at T-ball; I write on my sister-in-law's wall on Facebook to tell her that I just saw the cutest picture of our niece on Shutterfly. The permeability of the home that the Web and social networking enables, rather than eroding family life, is actually strengthening it. This is not the ideal nuclear family envisioned in the nineteenth and twentieth centuries in the West; rather, it is a revival of the old extended family, with mothers, sisters, and aunts all tweeting, sharing, and blogging, raising their families together online. All of this domesticity may give the impression that women are using Web 2.0 to uphold the patriarchy, and in many cases that may be true, but Mommy Blogging and social networking may also be

read as subverting the patriarchy. Rather than looking only to the father/
husband for guidance with the childrearing as in the Victorian or 1950s
Leave It to Beaver model, women and men are building networks of friends
and extended family with which they can share the process and look to
for guidance. Mommy Blogging, social networking, and other activities in
Web 2.0 are actually incredibly empowering for women.

Generally speaking, yes, the history of the Internet is a history of male
early adopters and then a colonization and domestication by women.
Happily, many aspects of this domestication, especially social networking,
have empowered women. Some of the early adopters of the Internet and
various Web applications have, however, been women. A parallel history
to that above is that of the female early adopter. Both histories are correct;
yet neither is complete without the other. From a theoretical standpoint,
it is not insignificant that women in the nineteenth century who were
employed to perform complex calculations were in fact called "computers." Sadie Plant, in her book *Zeros and Ones*, which seeks to reclaim
the place of women in the history of computing, makes great use of Ada
Lovelace. The daughter of Lord Byron, Lovelace used her background,
which afforded her much more freedom than the average young woman
in the 1840s, to study higher mathematics. Lovelace is celebrated by Plant
and widely credited by many as being the first computer programmer.
She wrote of the use of the punch cards of the Jacquard loom to program
Charles Babbage's Analytical Engine, which was either the first computer
or a very close relative to it. Women had a voice in computing technology from the beginning.

Pens and Needles

In "Pens and Needles," her keynote address to the 1993 meeting of the
American Quilt Study Group, Laurel Thatcher Ulrich noted a historic
tension, going back to the Renaissance, between the world of words and
scholarship (a traditionally male world) and the world of textiles (a traditionally female domain). The so-called woman question, a Renaissance-era
debate about the role of women in society, asked: Are women rational
and educable, and thus to be given the pen, or should women instead be
given the needle (implying that women are irrational and less educable)?[40]
Thus, it is somewhat ironic to have academic papers devoted to quilts as,
at least in the West, writing and the needle arts were imagined in binary
opposition to each other. Ulrich also noted that many textile scholars
(myself included) are word people rather than fabric people, and feel more

comfortable writing about quilts than they do making them. Indeed, several scholars of quilts and other needle arts have gone so far as to value the artistry of women's works, but they bemoan the fact that the women who made them were "forced" to sew all their lives.

Ulrich suggests that pens and needles, and the worlds of scholarship and stitchery that they embody, can be brought together by examining the eighteenth century, a period that Ulrich constructs as sitting as a sort of liminal point of time between the seventeenth century and Anne Bradstreet, America's first widely published female author, and the nineteenth century and the wild popularity of quilting. In the eighteenth century in America, the production of samplers, which often included stitched letters and/or numbers, was a common part of a girl's education. Also, fancy needlework created in the United States in the eighteenth century was made by literate women, and the bulk of American women's writing that was done before the middle of the eighteenth century survives not on paper but in needlework.[41] So, writing and needlework, *especially* in education, were quite connected in eighteenth-century America, perhaps more so than in twenty-first-century America.

Almost every nineteenth- and early twentieth-century literary magazine published short stories in which quilts were a major theme or motif. Women's magazines, such as *Godey's Lady's Book* and *Harper's Bazaar*, and regional farm magazines published quilt-related short stories as well. Cuesta Benberry, in her 1993 anthology, *A Patchwork of Pieces*, wrote that these stories tell us not only about trends or fashions in quilting and other needle arts of the times in which the stories were written but also about popular perceptions and attitudes toward quilters and quilts from a particular period.

An analysis of three quilt stories written in America in the 1870s, 1910s, and 1970s shows societal beliefs about quilts and women's lives; it also gives insight into major topics in the field of quilt studies, such as the art versus craft debate, and shows the interconnectedness of quilt studies with other disciplines, such as American studies and literary criticism. Elaine Showalter, in her essay "Common Threads," wrote that piecing and patchwork are both theme and form in women's writing.[42] Patchwork has come to symbolize a feminist aesthetic in visual (quilts) as well as written texts.

Louisa May Alcott's "moral bed quilt" tale for children from the 1870s, "Patty's Patchwork,"[43] gives insight into the ways in which quilting was a part of women's morality, girls' education, and the mourning process in the mid- to late nineteenth century. In the story, ten-year-old Patty has gone to stay with her spinster aunt while her mother is in the late stages of her pregnancy. Each day, before she may play, Patty's aunt requires her to work on her patchwork. The daily production of patchwork was standard in a young girl's day in America in this period; the diligence and usefulness of creating patchwork quilts was seen as crucial to a girl's moral education. When Patty's infant sister dies, infant mortality being another (all too) common part of daily life in this period, Patty works through her grief and turns her patchwork into a "moral bed quilt"[44] because she wants to be strong for her mother—to be, as she puts it, a "nice little comforter."[45] The idea of *being* a comforter equates quilt and quilter and suggests that the quilter, not only the quilt, possesses qualities of being warm and soothing. Patty's aunt notes that the patchwork quilt is metaphor for life itself, the light and dark patches of the quilt representing the joys and sorrows of daily life. It is also interesting to note that this story appeared in a collection of fiction for children by Alcott titled *Aunt Jo's Scrap Bag* (Jo referring to the character of Jo March from Alcott's classic novel *Little Women*). The scrap bag, a collection of random swatches of fabric, may be read as a metaphor for a collection of loosely related short stories.

Scholar Elaine Showalter has written that Susan Glaspell's story "A Jury of Her Peers,"[46] from the 1910s, may be read as a metaphor for feminist reading itself. In the story, a wife has just been accused of murdering her abusive husband, and the sheriff and his deputy search the couple's house and farm for clues to prove the wife's guilt. The sheriff's and deputy's wives accompany them to tidy the house. However, the wives come across a very erratic, chaotically pieced log cabin quilt. Such strange needlework, they realize, could only have been done by a very troubled mind. The wives rip out the stitches and redo the quilt, effectively destroying the only evidence of the accused woman's mania. Glaspell suggests a strong element of sisterhood here. The wives help a fellow woman in trouble even though they are, as the sheriff jokes, married to the law. When the sheriff and the deputy see their wives working on the quilt, they do not see them destroying the evidence in plain view; they can only comment that women are always interested in fabric and little trifles. Written during a time of agitation for women's suffrage and property rights, Glaspell criticizes what she sees as men's prejudice toward women's arts, including both quilting and women's writing. Men, Glaspell implies, think that women, in their quilting and writing, are only interested in trifles, not in lofty or important matters such as justice. Glaspell would have the reader think that men cannot read the language of the quilt, or see its maker's rage at her husband's abuse, just as they cannot truly understand women's writing. This quilt story points to a growing feminist consciousness in early twentieth-century America.

Finally, Alice Walker's story "Everyday Use,"[47] from the 1970s, says much about the role of historic quilts in modern society, feminism, and the African American consciousness from the period. In "Everyday Use," a hip, young, urban African American woman interested in pan-African ideas goes back to the Deep South to visit what she sees as her "backward" family. Dee, or Wangero, as she now prefers to be called, sees the family's heirloom quilts and wants to take them back to the city. The quilts are art to her, representing her African heritage, and she believes that they should be preserved on the wall. By contrast, her mother and sister Maggie, neither of whom ever received an education or left their small, rural community, see quilts as family heritage, to be used on the bed, and ultimately to be worn out. This is an interesting take on the art versus craft debate that has always been a part of quilt scholarship. Here, quilt as art takes on a sinister connotation, while quilt as craft takes on a positive connotation. Walker implies that quilts are a part of living culture and should be in use within the communities in which they were created, not taken back to New York and hung on the wall to forever be a static monument to their culture.

Access to Collaboration: Visual Searching and Pattern Recognition

So far in this chapter, we have discussed whimsical prints in fabrics, from snakes to postage stamps. Social taggings, tagging by AIs, and good metadata all help users who may be searching for snakes or stamps to access what they are looking for. But what of the user who is simply searching for whimsical prints, perhaps for inspiration for a creative project or maybe just for fun? If the user is familiar with the terms "novelty" and "conversation" or "conversational," then finding such prints using a text-based search is a snap. If, however, the user is not familiar with these terms, access becomes limited. In this instance, visual searching—returning visually similar images based on parameters such as color, line, pattern, and composition—could help to provide better access to images and their records. As with AI-assisted tagging, visual searching can be done by an algorithm "trained" to look for visual patterns. Similar technology is already in widespread use in applications like facial recognition.

A strictly visual search mechanism would be a boon in particular for the study of quilts, whose thousands of arcane pattern names are unfamiliar to all but the most avid quiltmakers and quilt historians. Two hundred of the most common pattern names—from "acorn" to "zig-zag"—are individually browsable on the Quilt Index (see chapter 1),[48] and Barbara Brackman names more than four thousand unique pieced quilt patterns in her *Encyclopedia of Pieced Quilt Patterns*[49] and more than two thousand appliqué patterns in *Encyclopedia of Appliqué*.[50] Wouldn't it be so much easier to click on a pattern and return results of visually similar patterns? Happily, visual searching is on the horizon for sites like Flickr and museum databases alike.

Visual Stylometry

Visual pattern recognition will soon be changing the ways in which we search for, understand, appreciate, and interact with works of art—including costume and textile objects. It is also changing the ways in which we research them. Perhaps ironically to some, technological means are now being used to authenticate original works of art, and the computer will ultimately prove a better connoisseur than even the most practiced human eye.

> We now find ourselves at a point where it may be possible to bring to bear many new mathematical ideas on the analysis of art and the particular problem that underlies authentication—that of the quantification of artistic style. The "problem" of style quantification is one that is well-posed generally throughout the arts, whether it be in literature, music, or the visual arts. It finds its roots in the search for methods for quantifying literary style, a challenge that was first stated at least as far back as 1854 by the mathematician Augustus De Morgan. In 1897 the term *stylometry* [original] was coined by the historian of philosophy, Wincenty Lutaslowski, as a catch-all for a collection of statistical techniques applied to questions of authorship and evolution of style in the literary arts.[51]

In the article "EMD Analysis for Visual Stylometry," a team of mathematicians from Michigan State University, Dartmouth College, and the Santa Fe Institute put forward a model for machine intelligence in the identification of authorship for artistic works. Again, we find a convergence of quilts and mathematics in the digital age. Using paintings and drawings by the Northern Renaissance artist Pieter Bruegel the Elder (ca. 1525/1530–1569) as their test case, Dong Mao, Daniel Rockmore, Yang Wang, and Qiang Wu used empirical mode decompression (EMD) to determine whether works were indeed created by Bruegel the Elder. The key feature of EMD is the feature vector, a multidimensional vector made up of values that stand for aspects of a particular type of a work of art.[52] As a simplified example, one might let C = color, B = brushstroke, and so on, for a vector that would read, "[*C*, *B* . . .]." The computer learns to work with the feature vector over time. This machine learning process involves a learning set, in which the computer is given a set of paintings to identify, some of which are obviously Bruegel's—that is, they exhibit many of the features that are unique to Bruegel's painting style in terms of brushstrokes, color palette, and so on—and some that are obviously not by Bruegel, very different works perhaps not even by a Northern Renaissance painter. Once the computer has mastered this learning set, works to be authenticated are tested against known works by Bruegel. Similar projects using different techniques, including fractal-based authentication (Jackson Pollock), wavelet-based authentication (Vincent van Gogh), and sparse coding, have been conducted by other research projects.[53] "In the case of visual media, while all analysis derives from pixel information, there are a much wider range of first order analytic tools from which the classifiers are built (e.g., pixel information, Fourier spectra, wavelet spectra, etc.) so that in short, there is much less agreement on the fundamental analytic elements and the search for and development of new analytic tools for classification is ongoing."[54] There has been some controversy over whether these other techniques for visual analysis are as accurate as EMD.

High-performance computing (computing beyond the power of any current desktop computer) is now in use by scholars at Michigan State University, the University of Sheffield in the United Kingdom, and the University of Illinois at Urbana-Champaign to answer questions about large masses of visual data. The Quilt Index's Digging Into Data project and the use of visual stylometry to answer humanities questions about the more than fifty thousand (and counting) quilts held in the index's database is yet another example of the vast opportunities for new directions in scholarship created by textile collections online. Visual stylometry will allow for the scalability of the Quilt Index in the face of massive amounts of quilt data, enabling scholars and quiltmakers to make new meaning out of a vast collection of quilts. The technique could also help to ascertain cultural authorship. For example, visual stylometry could identify quilts made by the Indiana or Illinois Amish, who choose their fabrics from a dark and distinctive color palette, from those made by Pennsylvania Amish. Visual stylometry also has the potential for the identification of individual makers through analysis of minute visual details, such as quilting stitches per inch, in addition to communities of makers (which can be identified on the basis of pattern and fabric choices).

The authentication of individuals' styles in traditional quiltmaking will begin to break down the binary between traditional quilts and art quilts, and between form and function in quiltmaking. At the same time, however, the ideological shift from individual authorship to cultural authorship precipitated by digital reproduction and advanced by social technologies such as crowdsourcing and social tagging is very much in line with the traditionally communal ethos of quiltmaking. According to textile artist Ingrid Bachmann, "What is at stake in the scripting of technologies as old, new, hot, cold, authored, anonymous? And what is at stake with the dismantling of the frontier myth of digital technology? . . . We are reminded that even in our newest technologies we remain firmly rooted in the structures of the past."[55] Visual stylometry of quiltmaking, in contrast to painting, reveals both communal and individual accomplishment and identity, tradition, and future technology.

Women and Cyborgs

In "Five Decades of Popular Cybernetics," Paasonen notes that the prefix *cyber*, as in cyberspace, cyberculture, and cyberfeminism, has come to mean something much different in the English language than its etymology would suggest. The origin of this popular prefix comes from the word *cybernetics*, meaning "the science of communications and automatic control in machines and organic systems, and the study of messages in controlling machinery and society."[56] This definition is taken from the writing of Norbert Wiener, the "father" of cybernetics.

There is yet another body of work and theory on cybernetics, popular cybernetics, which focuses on popular conceptions of the cyborg, especially as they are imagined in the popular media. It is from ideas of popular cybernetics that characters such as the Bionic Woman, the Stepford Wives, and Rosie, the robotic yet loving maid in the animated series *The Jetsons*, have sprung. It is not insignificant that all of these are female characters. Of course, there are several examples of male cyborgs, often action heroes that may be culled from television, film, and the pages of comic books. As Susanna Paasonen has noted, however, the historical objectification of women makes the feminine particularly interesting and appealing as cyborg. "Female automata—women as machines and machines as ideal women—have been imagined since at least the eighteenth century. The figure of the woman-machine has been used to articulate the machine-like nature of the human, perhaps since the category of woman has been historically objectified (as dolls, machines, servants) in different ways than that of man."[57] Women, doing physical work in tandem with a digital, networked sewing machine, having embodied interactions in cyberspace, may be read then as female automata. Terms such as *cyborg* and *automaton* are grounded in social and technological histories that are, in one important way, very much different from life in the present age. Both of these ideas—the cyborg and the automaton—were conceived before the widespread popular use of digital technologies and networked computing.

In his 1964 book, *Understanding the Media: New Extensions of Man*, media theorist Marshall McLuhan wrote that technology is simply anything that is an "extension or self-amputation of our physical bodies."[58] From bifocals and breast implants to titanium golf clubs and sewing machines, people have been using technology to enhance their bodies or the functions that their bodies can perform for hundreds of years. While bifocals and sewing machines certainly seem harmless enough, advances in biotechnology, media representations of cyborgs such as the Bionic Woman and the Terminator, and the rapidly shrinking gap in the human–computer interface brought about by technologies such as voice and fingerprint recognition have some scholars proposing that the twenty-first-century human is actually a humachine.

Mark Poster wrote of a real newness in *Information Please*, something that is radically different about the relations between humans, nature, society, and technology, and this is, of course, digital technology and networked computing. Given the significant changes in cultural relations that this technological shift has brought about, Poster uses the book, in his own words, "to pinpoint the places where cultural theory would benefit from alteration and revision by attention to new relations of humans and information machines."[59] Central to these alterations and revisions is Poster's concept of the humachine, the idea that the twenty-first-century human (in the developed world) relies upon digital technology as an amplification of the body in order to complete tasks basic to humanity, such as communication, at all times.

Women and Mathematics

This section explores the role of mathematics and education in access to the digital (often via textiles). The shared binary nature of computing and electrical systems, and woven textiles and Babbage's and Lovelace's use of the punch cards of the Jacquard loom in computer programming are but two of the myriad examples of the intersections of quilts and other textiles with mathematics, electricity, and computer science. For example, in Paul J. Nahin's 2009 work on mathematical physics, *Mrs. Perkins's Electric Quilt*, Nahin devotes an entire chapter, "Quilts and Electricity," to the role that quilts play and have played in recreational mathematics. According to

Nahin, in a 1907 issue of *Our Puzzle Magazine*, Sam Lloyd published the original quilt-related mathematical quandary:

> A square quilt of 169 identical square patches (that is, the quilt is thirteen patches by thirteen patches) is to be cut into a number of pieces which are themselves to be square by cutting along the stitch lines [in the ditch]. In other words, you are not allowed to cut through a patch. How can this be done in the fewest number of subsquares?[60]

Henry Dudeney's book *Amusements in Mathematics* (1917) reprinted the puzzle, calling the division of a square into subsquares a "Mrs. Perkins's Quilt." Interestingly enough, this mathematical problem was named after the fictitious Mrs. Potipher Perkins, a name invented by Dudeney for its folksy and whimsical qualities, qualities that he desired to ascribe to his recreational mathematical puzzles.[61] Thus, we see the use of quilts in geometry for two reasons: the inherent geometric complexities of quilt squares, and the ability of quilts and the culture of quilting to produce an idea of warmth that softens the supposed coldness of mathematics.

It is due to both quilts' geometry and their warmth and approachability that they have also been used extensively in K–16 mathematical education. Math teachers who also quilt abound. Two sources for mathematical quilts for educational uses are Diana Venters and Elaine Krajenke Ellison's *Mathematical Quilts: No Sewing Required!* (1999)[62] and *More Mathematical Quilts: No Sewing Required!* (2003).[63] Mathematical concepts demonstrated through quilts in these books include the Golden Ratio and Fibonacci Sequence, spirals, tessellations, fractals, right triangles, the Pythagorean theorem, and many other ideas. However, even today, many curricular materials that aim to engage girls with mathematics through quilts and other textiles are unsuccessful because they promote, rather than condemn, gender stereotypes that function to distance women from the sphere of math and technology. According to Mary Harris, author of *Common Threads: Women, Mathematics and Work*:

> They [publications that appear to aim to link textiles and mathematics] fail because they maintain the stereotype of textiles work as something without intellect, upon which mathematics can be imposed thereby giving it value it did not previously have. Such work contains no recognition of any inherent mathematics in the making or the use of the textiles and the message that mathematics is something separate and superior to the textiles activity is usually clear. Such publications often sell themselves as "girl-friendly" with the gendered and patronising message along the lines of "Look girls, here is something serious you can do with your pretty stuff."[64]

Recognizing the intellectual component of textiles in mathematics and mathematics through textiles is key to understanding the role of textiles in a digital age.

FIBERSPACE. For example, a *fiberspace*, a Seifert fiberspace to be exact, is a term in hyperbolic geometry for a kind of three-manifold. In his book *Outer Circles: An Introduction to Hyperbolic 3-Manifolds* (2007), Albert Marden explains the fiberspace through an equation, $M^3 = R \times S^1$.

> An example of a Seifert fiber space, or Seifert manifold, is given by $M^3 = R \times S^1$, with R a compact surface; the boundary components of R, if any, become incompressible boundary tori for M^3. Other examples are obtained by replacing a finite number of circles in M^3 with "singular fibers"; a singular fiber has a neighborhood homeomorphic to the quotient of $D \times S^1$ of $D \times R$ under the action $(z, t) \mid \rightarrow (wz, t + 1/q)$, where w is a primitive q-th root of unity and D is the open unit disk centered at $z = 0$. Each nonsingular fiber wraps q-times around the singular one. An orientable M^3 is called a Seifert fibered if it is a union of pairwise disjoint simple loops, each with a closed neighborhood, a union of fibers, which is fiber-homeomorphic to a fibered solid torus $D \times S^1$ as described above.[65]

Several other advanced geometrical concepts with names that have a connection etymologically to textiles, including "spinning," "singular fibers," and "fibering over the circle," are discussed by Marden as well.

In the West, mathematics has been constructed as a male endeavor, while needlework and the textile arts have been gendered as female. This is related to the idea of the educability of women (and the perceived lack thereof) that led to the "pens and needles" division of labor discussed in the previous chapter, and this bifurcation belies the common thread connecting the pursuits of mathematics and textiles, the logic or systematicity of the binary. A logical system cannot function only with either male or female, zero or one. Ada Lovelace was able to leverage her family's money and privileged situation to do advanced work in mathematics, work informed by an understanding of woven fabrics. Historically, many women have been less fortunate.

A relatively new branch of cultural anthropology,[66] ethnomathematics, explores alternative mathematics, ways of knowing, using, and doing mathematics outside Western academic mathematics. Harris proposes that the mathematics of textiles be viewed through the disciplinary lens of ethnomathematics.

> Ethnomathematics is that "which is practised among identifiable cultural groups such as national-tribal societies, labor groups, children of a certain

age-bracket, professional classes, and so on" (D'Ambrosio 1991). Under such a definition, the academic mathematics of institutional education, and the mathematics of women who sew, are both examples of ethnomathematics among many (Harris 1987). The institutionalisation of one elite ethnomathematics at the end of the nineteenth century, and its world spread, effectively devalued all others then and since.[67]

Ada Lovelace's seminal idea of "weaving the digital" was conceived at the intersection of these two ethnomathematical systems, nineteenth-century British academic mathematics and what Harris calls "the mathematics of women who sew."

Weaving Algebraic Patterns

The digital, or binary, nature of textiles is a simple, but very important, point of departure for scholarship on textiles and technology. Further, digital textile culture often exists at the intersection of other binaries, such as male and female, art and craft, and technology and textile. Cybercultural theorist Sadie Plant views these binary oppositions as an indication that human *techne* and *episteme* are really just complex machine processes. Textile artist and theorist Ingrid Bachmann explores these binaries through a study of discourse and rhetoric. In her essay "Material and the Promise of the Immaterial," one of many works that examine the inherent connections between textiles and the digital, including the binary nature of each, as well as their once joint history in the use of the punch cards of the Jacquard loom in the programming of the first protocomputer, the Analytical Engine, Bachmann asks,

> What is the gap between a technology's apparent role, history, perceived use, its expected user, and its actual role, function and history? Why is weaving considered antiquated, artisanal, slow, gendered female? Conversely, why are computers considered fast, new, state of the art, virtual, gendered male? The currency or, more accurately, lack of currency of textiles as a technology is rather pointedly illustrated in a recent advertisement in *Wired* magazine for an Internet provider. In the ad, a sexy redhead poses provocatively against a computer. The accompanying copy reads, "Let's just say that you won't find me on the knitting newsgroup." Clearly, knitting is for doddering old grandmothers, not for foxy cyberbabes or hip infobahn warriors.[68]

One of the major projects of this book has been to deconstruct such binaries and dispel many of these gendered myths. Women, including young women, are actively engaged in a plethora of craft-related activities online.

Indeed, many young women became early adopters of the Internet in the 1990s *because* of their desire to join others in spaces such as the sorts of quilting and knitting newsgroups about which the advertisement so derisively jeered. Further, textiles *are* technologies, and vice versa.

Significantly, the first protocomputer program was born from the translation of warp and weft to zero and one in the punch cards of the Jacquard loom. When Ada Lovelace translated the Italian engineer Menbrea's paper on the Analytical Engine and its programming, she wrote in her extensive notes to the translation of the Analytical Engine *weaving algebraic patterns*.[69] The inner functioning of the first computer was conceived of as a kind of weaving. The metaphor of technological process as needlecraft technique works on many levels, from the weaving of code to the motherboard or database as an intricate tapestry to the idea of online communities as being woven, stitched, or quilted together.

The Future of Access: Linked Data

Tim Berners-Lee is the English computer scientist who is often credited as "the man who invented the Internet." What he actually invented in the late 1980s was hypertext transfer protocol (HTTP), a common vernacular that allowed for communications between computers using standardized addresses, or URLs. These days, Berners-Lee is an advocate for another common vernacular, one that he thinks will be just as pivotal as HTTP and URL in the history of information access online. As we have seen, databases often exist as silos. Data in one silo cannot easily be cross-referenced with that in another, not only because they may use different metadata sets but also because they are simply not linked together. In his TED Talks "The Next Web of Open Linked Data"[70] and "The Year Open Data Went Worldwide" (with its chant of "raw data now!"),[71] Berners-Lee explains that linked open data, or simply linked data, uses resource description framework, RDF, and URIs (uniform resource identifiers) instead of URLs to provide a structured data format in which databases created in different metadata schemes can still communicate with each other and other data on the Internet.[72] Semantically, structured data works on the basis of what are referred to as triples: subject, object, and predicate. Data here is about relationships, and the data lies in how individual objects, persons, or events are related to each other. A simple and fairly banal example of this is "Halston likes orchids," in which Halston is the subject, orchids the object, and likes the predicate. This statement can be written out and rendered as a sentence in a static webpage (the Web 1.0 way of putting information online), written as a comment on a friend's blog or social network site (as in Web 2.0), or rendered as linked data through URIs that define each aspect of the triple. For example, "Halston likes orchids" could be expressed <https://en.wikipedia.org/wiki/Halston> <https://en.wikipedia.org/wiki/Orchidaceae> <https://www.facebook.com/help/452446998120360/>.

In this example, *Wikipedia* pages on Halston and Orchids provide a context for subject and object, while Facebook's help page on the practice of liking provides a context for the predicate. One may also come across the term FOAF, the acronym for "friend of a friend," which is another machine-readable way for describing the relationships specifically between people. FOAF effectively eliminates the need for the use of a database at all.

To be a good citizen in a world of linked data, Berners-Lee suggests (1) making your (or your institution's) collection's data available on the Web, (2) making it available as structured data, (3) using a nonproprietary format, for example, using .csv (comma separated values) file extension instead of Microsoft's spreadsheet program, Excel, and (4) using URIs to identify things, so that anyone can easily access your collection's information. Several museums have already published their collections' databases in an alternate format as open linked data. There is even a scholarly network of museum professionals with a strong interest in linked data: LODLAM (Linked Open Data in Libraries, Archives, and Museums).[73] What would happen if more museums made their collections' data available to the public in this way? In "Radically Open Cultural Heritage Data on the Web," given at Museums and the Web in 2012, Jon Voss offered ideas about what museum professionals might actually *do* in a future of linked museum data:

> As you develop new online projects, think about how Linked Open Data could be incorporated to improve your project. If you're curating an online exhibit on a WWI battalion for instance, think about how you could visualize data about other battalions, or draw on content from other institutions about this particular battalion. Think of how you might browse your online collections interactively, based on keywords or semantic terms that draw out connections that might not have been obvious. While the implementation may be out of reach at the moment, it's exactly these kinds of creative use cases that will help us keep pushing the boundaries and make the web of data a reality.[74]

As more museums put linked data online, more connections between disparate objects can be made. New discoveries about makers, materials, and techniques are bound to happen. Exhibitions and education work will also be enriched.

The social Web is fast becoming the semantic Web, a World Wide Web made up of linked data as opposed to webpages. This will provide unprecedented access not to information written up and nicely presented in webpages but to raw collections data, allowing for scholarly and design-related uses that we probably cannot even yet imagine. Chapter 3 takes a step back from this unfolding future of the Internet to look at the Web's present, and specifically how individuals are using social sites to curate collections of historic dress online.

Notes

1. Joe Queenan, "Still Life with Badly Dressed Museum-Goer," *Wall Street Journal* (August 27, 2015), http://www.wsj.com/articles/museums-crack-down-on-your-badly-dressed-visitors-1440691602.

2. Queenan.

3. W. Logan Fry, "Fiber in Cyberspace," *FiberArts* 27 (January/February 2001): 40–41.

4. Roland Jackson, "The Virtual Visit: Towards a New Concept for the Electronic Science Centre," in *Museums in a Digital Age*, ed. Ross Parry (London: Routledge, 2010), 155.

5. Marissa Fessenden, "Computers Are Learning about Art Faster than Art Historians," *Smithsonian Magazine* (May 2015), http://www.smithsonianmag.com/smart-news/computers-are-getting-better-identifying-artists-art-historians-are-180955241/#aZ6yd84bC3eSt0id.99.

6. Fessenden.

7. Flickr: The Commons, https://www.flickr.com/commons.

8. Flickr: Creative Commons, https://www.flickr.com/creativecommons/.

9. Search for "LACMA" and "Public Domain," Flickr: The Commons, https://www.flickr.com/search/?tags=lacma&license=7%2C9%2C10.

10. As a visiting assistant professor, I am not eligible for institutional support to pay for image permissions despite being a full-time faculty member.

11. Reptilian Fabric—The National Archives UK, Flickr Commons, https://www.flickr.com/photos/nationalarchives/3208858799/in/photolist-5TyeVH-oet65D-otUXhY-oxGpoz-oesmLx-ovEVjR-oesvtU-ovEGdR-ovK1uf-oesPum-ovWD2H-oesfJm-otVfpo-oesr14-oerGKy-ovXtxk-oesB2r-oesWEH-ovX9hX-ovVdqY-ovVw2u-ovX74Z-otUYU5-oerD5s-ovESzc.

12. I have added the English translations from the German—only the German terms appear as tags on the actual website.

13. Reptilian Fabric—The National Archives UK.

14. Nicholas Frankel, "The Ecstasy of Decoration: The Grammar of Ornament as Embodied Experience," *Nineteenth Century Art Worldwide* 2, no. 1 (2003): 1–32.

15. New York Fashion Week Live, http://newyorkfashionweeklive.com/instagram.

16. Olivia Fleming, "Why the World's Most Talked-About New Art Dealer Is Instagram," *Vogue* (May 13, 2014), http://www.vogue.com/872448/buying-and-selling-art-on-instagram/.

17. Vanessa Rosales and Ariele Elia, "Instagram and Fashion," public lecture given at the Fashion Institute of Technology (FIT) Museum, New York City, October 8, 2015.

18. Google Art Project, https://www.google.com/culturalinstitute/project/art-project.

19. Amit Sood, "Building a Museum of Museums on the Web," TED Talks (March 2011), https://www.ted.com/talks/amit_sood_building_a_museum_of_museums_on_the_web?language=en.

20. "The Harvesters," Google Cultural Institute, https://www.google.com/culturalinstitute/asset-viewer/the-harvesters/PAH1oMZ5dGBkxg?projectId=art-project.

21. International Quilt Study Center & Museum, Google Cultural Institute, https://www.google.com/culturalinstitute/collection/international-quilt-study-center-museum?projectId=art-project.

22. "Quilt Explorer," International Quilt Study Center & Museum, http://www.quiltstudy.org/collections/quilt_explorer.html.

23. "World Quilts: The American Story," International Quilt Study Center & Museum, http://worldquilts.quiltstudy.org/americanstory/.

24. Tapestry, http://tapestry.philau.edu.

25. About—Tapestry, http://tapestry.philau.edu/about/#sthash.0BkN3ilB.dpuf.

26. Nobuko Kajitani, "Care of Fabrics in the Museum," in *Changing Views of Textile Conservation*, eds. Mary M. Brooks and Dinah D. Eastop (Los Angeles: Getty Conservation Institute, 2011), 88.

27. 1975—Search Results—Tapestry, http://tapestry.philau.edu/?s=1975.

28. 1996.116.36—Tapestry, http://tapestry.philau.edu/1996–116–36/.

29. Richard Fisher and Dorothy Wolfthal, *Textile Print Design* (Fairchild Books and Visuals, 1987), 68.

30. Andie Robertson, "Interpreting the Woven Devoré Textile," in *The Future of the 20th Century: Collecting, Interpreting and Conserving Modern Materials*, eds. Cordelia Rogerson and Paul Garside (London: Archetype, 2006), 18.

31. Robertson, 18.

32. Robertson, 22.

33. Robertson, 23.

34. Shelley Bernstein et al., "Brooklyn Museum Collection, Posse, and Tag! You're It!" (paper presented at the annual conference on Museums and the Web, Indianapolis, Indiana, April 15–18, 2009).

35. For a more lengthy discussion on the Internet as the Wild West, see Ted Friedman's *Electric Dreams* (New York: New York University Press, 2005).

36. Susanna Paasonen, *Figures of Fantasy: Internet, Women and Cyberdiscourse* (New York: Peter Lang, 2005), 131.

37. Friedman, 171, 174.

38. Joanna Turney, *The Culture of Knitting* (Oxford: Berg, 2009), 151.

39. Mark Poster, *Information Please: Culture and Politics in the Age of Digital Machines* (Durham, NC: Duke University Press, 2006), 171–73.

40. Laurel Thatcher Ulrich, "Pens and Needles: Documents and Artifacts in Women's History," *Uncoverings* 14 (1993): 221.

41. Ulrich, 223–24.

42. Elaine Showalter, "Common Threads," in *Sister's Choice: Tradition and Change in American Women's Writing* (New York: Oxford University Press, 1991), 149, 169.

43. Louisa May Alcott, "Patty's Patchwork," in *Aunt Jo's Scrap Bag* (Boston: Roberts Brothers, 1889), 193–215.

44. Alcott, 210.

45. Alcott, 215.

46. Susan Glaspell, "A Jury of Her Peers," http://www.learner.org/interactives/literature/story/fulltext.html.

47. Alice Walker, "Everyday Use," Crossroads—University of Virginia, http://xroads.virginia.edu/~ug97/quilt/walker.html.

48. "Browse by Category: Pattern," the Quilt Index, http://www.quiltindex.org/browsepattern.php.

49. Barbara Brackman, *Encyclopedia of Pieced Quilt Patterns* (Paducah, KY: American Quilter's Society, 1993).

50. Barbara Brackman, *Encyclopedia of Appliqué* (Lafayette, CA: C&T Publishing, 2009).

51. Dong Mao, Daniel N. Rockmore, Yang Wang, and Qiang Wu, "EMD Analysis for Visual Stylometry," *IEEE Transactions on Pattern Analysis and Machine Intelligence*, http://www.mth.msu.edu/~ywang/Preprints/EMD_Bruegel-IEEE.pdf, 1.

52. Mao et al., 6.

53. Mao et al., 2.

54. Mao et al., 1.

55. Ingrid Bachmann, "Material and the Promise of the Immaterial," in *Material Matters: The Art and Culture of Contemporary Textiles*, eds. Ingrid Bachmann and Ruth Scheuing (Toronto: YYZ Books, 1998), 33.

56. Susanna Paasonen, *Figures of Fantasy: Internet, Women and Cyberdiscourse* (New York: Peter Lang, 2005), 11.

57. Paasonen, 46.

58. Marshall McLuhan quoted in Paasonen, 52.

59. Poster, 4.

60. Paul J. Nahin, *Mrs. Perkins's Electric Quilt and Other Intriguing Stories of Mathematical Physics* (Princeton, NJ: Princeton University Press, 2009), 215–16.

61. Nahin, 216.

62. Diana Venters and Elaine Krajenke Ellison, *Mathematical Quilts: No Sewing Required!* (Emeryville, CA: Key Curriculum Press, 1999).

63. Diana Venters and Elaine Krajenke Ellison, *More Mathematical Quilts: No Sewing Required!* (Emeryville, CA: Key Curriculum Press, 2003).

64. Mary Harris, *Common Threads: Women, Mathematics and Work* (Stoke on Trent, UK: Trentham Books, 1997), 111.

65. Albert Marden, *Outer Circles: An Introduction to Hyperbolic 3-Manifolds* (Cambridge: Cambridge University Press, 2007), 328.

66. Harris, 195.

67. Harris, 195.

68. Bachmann, 25.

69. James Essinger, *Jacquard's Web: How a Hand-loom Led to the Birth of the Information Age* (Oxford: Oxford University Press, 2004), 141.

70. Tim Berners-Lee, "The Next Web of Open Linked Data," TED Talks (February 2009), http://www.youtube.com/watch?v=OM6XIICm_qo.

71. Tim Berners-Lee, "The Year Open Data Went Worldwide," TED Talks (February 2010), http://www.youtube.com/watch?v=3YcZ3Zqk0a8.

72. See also Linked Data, http://linkeddata.org.

73. LODLAM, Linked Open Data in Libraries, Archives, and Museums, http://lodlam.net.

74. Jon Voss, "Radically Open Cultural Heritage Data on the Web," Museums and the Web (2012), http://www.museumsandtheweb.com/mw2012/papers/radically_open_cultural_heritage_data_on_the_w.

Curation   3

USAN SONTAG ONCE SAID THAT STYLE IS "the principle of decision
in a work of art."[1] Most people, while they might not buy designer
labels, have their own innate sense of style in selecting and combining
pieces of clothing and accessories to wear each day. Museum curators, too,
display their own personal curatorial style in the choices that they make:
themes for exhibitions, works put on exhibit, meaningful juxtapositions.
While most everyone can be trusted to curate their own wardrobe, relatively few people—those with years of graduate school behind them—are
trusted to curate the history of dress in museums. But, since everyone has
some innate sense of style, some means of making decisions about combining works of art into a more or less cohesive whole, what would happen
if clothing and textile objects were curated outside the museum setting by
people without an advanced degree?

Increasingly, on social websites like Tumblr and Polyvore, individual
users *are* curating such objects. On Polyvore, these curatorial creations
are called "collections" and combine historic fashion photographs and
magazine layouts with contemporary dress and textile objects. This chapter
explores this growing trend toward user-curation online, with a focus on
user-curated collections of mid-twentieth-century fashion, such as "Audrey Hepburn on the Moon"[2] (see figure 3.1). Everyday people with an
interest in design, fashion, or crafts are organizing objects both for their
own inspiration and to share with others. Those who work in dress and
textile collections can learn a lot from the themes and juxtapositions created by people outside the museum's walls. Indeed, the Internet has proved
an interesting laboratory in which museum staff can sit back and watch

Figure 3.1.   Polyvore collection: "Audrey Hepburn on the Moon." Created by Coco Mault.

what happens when people who aren't professional historians curate collections. The results, as we will see, are rich and exciting.

This chapter begins with two case studies of ways in which users are curating historic dress (especially couture of the 1960s and 1970s) collections on two very different online social sites: Polyvore and Tumblr. With these collections and blogs underpinning the discussion, the bulk of the chapter explores key changes occurring in museum practice today. "User-Curation, Museums, and the Participatory Web" unpacks this new tendency toward the sharing of curatorial authority while offering critical perspectives on the value of user-curated content in the museum, including what we as museum professionals can learn from these new curatorial practices. This section also explores the ever-changing nature of the curatorial process and what exactly it means for people, especially young people, to participate in the arts. The chapter concludes with six tenets of user-curation in museums.

Polyvore

Polyvore[3] is a social application in which users can create and share fashion and interior design ideas with others. Originally intended as a social shopping site, it has quickly become much more—a design tool for those with interests in fashion, fabric, or design that, like Pinterest, allows users to showcase objects and images of interest but, in addition, lets them control the presentation of those objects with user-friendly, Web-based design software. Further, while Polyvore is not a Facebook app and is independent of Facebook, it makes use of users' existing social networks by interfacing seamlessly with Facebook. This makes it easy for a person's friends and fellow fashion enthusiasts to see their creations.

Polyvore, as its name suggests, consumes from multiples sources, drawing the bulk of the objects available for user collections from a large bank of retail websites (tending toward high-end retail sites like Net-a-Porter), along with direct-from-the-maker sites such as Etsy. Polyvore also pulls images from vintage fashion photography, fashion magazines, and runway reports, as well as other participating collections, such as archives and museums (especially museum shops). Users search for items by type (e.g., caftan), color, or keyword, such as "Loulou de la Falaise" or "Halston" or "sequins." Once the user has found an item that they wish to use, they drag it into their collage space, where they can combine found objects with text, patterns, frames, and other graphic elements. Collections are shared with friends and found by other users via keyword search.

Curating the 1960s

Clothing styles from the 1960s are some of the most easily recognizable to contemporary eyes. Subcultural uniforms of the mods and hippies, as well as Space Age, Op and Pop, and ethnic influences, are familiar garb of the period, even to those born long after the decade.[4] Indeed, with its emphasis on youth, rebellion, and collective action, the 1960s have tremendous appeal for young people today. While many users create Polyvore collections that are quite contemporary, vintage collections and especially collections based around the 1960s are also very popular. "Swinging London,"[5] a collection about historic Carnaby Street created for the Polyvore 1960s Challenge, and "Twiggy"[6] were both created by Foxboro. Each collection expresses an understanding of the design sensibility of the 1960s (even though the curator was almost certainly not yet born in the 1960s) and re creates that aesthetic using contem porary objects. Effectively, these function as small, curated, historical exhibits.

Donyale Luna, Detroit-born model, actress, and society "it-girl" of the 1960s, has been the subject of numerous Polyvore collections. In a collection by Lilysue, a photograph of Luna on the cover of *Vogue* is juxtaposed with contemporary luxe pieces by Missoni and edited by Satinee—Georges

Hobeika.[7] AlexD, another Polyvore user, curated a different collection around Donyale Luna. The accompanying text, which for our purposes can be taken as the analog of an object label, reads, "Donyale Luna was one of the worlds most beautiful women in the 1960s. She began modeling in 1965, & was the first black model to appear in British Vogue."[8] A college student with an interest in the history of women of color in fashion, AlexD has also curated collections on black fashion icons June Ambrose and Dorothea Towles.[9]

In a similar vein, another user asks through their Polyvore collection, "Marianne Faithfull inspired,"[10] "Do you remember the 60s?" In this collection, the user-curator, Vlg-Budde, combines a vintage swing dress from the 1960s, modeled by singer and actress Marianne Faithfull, with contemporary pieces, noting that they represent "a modern aproach [sic] to the same colors and style." The text accompanying the collection reads, "Another muse to the Rolling Stones and Mick Jagger's ex-girlfriend, singer Marianne Faithfull lived a wild life (reportedly answering the door to the police dressed in a rug after taking drugs), but she always looked effortlessly cool in her wardrobe of mini-dresses, fur coats and knee-high boots."[11]

Significantly, both AlexD and Vlg-Budde's pseudo-object labels are quite good, museologically speaking. In Ambrose and Paine's *Museum Basics*, a primer on the museum profession, the authors explain how to write a good object label. One of the keys, they say, is keeping the label intelligible for the reader while still providing enough pertinent information.

> Most museum texts and labels are much too complicated. They are written by specialists who know a great deal about their subject and about the objects, and who sometimes forget that most of their visitors will know very little about either. . . . On the other hand, some museum labels are much too simple. A label reading "old plough given by Hilda Beckenham" is quite useless.[12]

Both AlexD and Vlg-Budde have achieved a good balance of ease of reading with information. Ambrose and Paine also note the ideal length of an object label: less than 150 words is good, but around 50 words is best.[13] AlexD's label on the Donyale Luna collections is twenty-nine words long, while Vlg-Budde's label on the Marianne Faithfull collection is forty-seven words. Lay curators can be surprisingly effective in not only selecting themes and objects but also conveying relatable information.

"Style Inspiration: Anita Pallenberg"[14] is a collection curated by Bohemians based on German-Italian actress, model, and 1960s fashion icon

Anita Pallenberg. The collection comprises contemporary clothing pieces, including a skirt from Miu Miu, closely matched to vintage photographs of Pallenberg. Users can allow open commenting on their collections, and this is a way for curators of these collections to make the curatorial experience more social, getting feedback and validation from friends and other users who have stumbled across their collections. For example, Fiendishthingy writes, "Great match! I adore Anita and her sense of fashion."[15]

Indeed, Pallenberg is renowned for her sense of style, and when asked whether style is something one is just born with (or not), or whether it can be learned, she replied, "Style has nothing to do with consumerism and money. I have had lots of money at points in my life, but I never went to Dior or anything like that. I'd rather hunt it down in secondhand shops. The pleasure of finding something I've found that I like is infinitely more pleasurable than having a whole wardrobe presented to you by a stylist."[16] The dichotomy of personally thrifted couture versus a wardrobe curated by a professional stylist is an apt metaphor for the difference between the user-curated collections of Polyvore and the polished, professional exhibitions of dress found in museums. People like to curate their own collections because they, like the professionals, derive pleasure from the hunt, scrolling through pages and pages of objects in Polyvore's database to find just the right object. Museum exhibitions are undoubtedly more *professional*, but user-curated exhibitions are much more *personal*.

The Power of User-Curation

Why should we care about how (presumably) young people curate the history of dress online? This intimately personal quality of user-curated collections has tremendous applications for museum learning. In *Learning from Museums: Visitor Experiences and the Making of Meaning*, John Falk and Lynn Dierking note that learning takes place in personal, sociocultural, and physical contexts.[17] Like personal style, which is deeply rooted in the wearer's sense of self—their "beliefs, heritage, culture, dreams, lifestyle and community"[18]—the personal context for learning (within or outside the museum) largely revolves around the learner's sense of self. "Learning is not just facts and concepts; learning, particularly intrinsically motivated learning, is a rich, emotion-laden experience, encompassing much, if not most, of what we consider to be fundamentally human. At its most basic level, learning is about affirming *self* [emphasis in original]."[19] By engaging in the curatorial process, by making choices about the themes and objects that matter to them and appeal to their eye, user-curators on Polyvore are not only teaching others about their favorite style and fashion icons but also learning much about their own aesthetic sensibilities and connections to history.

The potential uses for Polyvore by dress and textile collections are vast. Museum staff can combine "objects of the day" from other social media channels into thematic tableaus based on user feedback. Users could create their own Polyvore collections based on objects in the museum's collection, or combine objects from one's own museum collection with those held at other institutions. These are merely a few examples that illustrate the possibilities that a design-based social media platform offers. Besides the traditional social media applications, museums with collections of twentieth-century dress can use Polyvore in educational programming. The image bank on Polyvore is replete with designer objects, both vintage and contemporary, making the site useful for user-curated historical dress studies.

The site has potential for teaching and research applications as well. For example, I created a collection of Byzantine-inspired jewelry by Jade Jagger alongside a Byzantine-Russian icon—the Black Madonna of Częsttochowa, from the Jasna Góra Monastery in Częstochowa, Poland— for the Byzantine lecture in my design history course (see figure 3.2), and I made a collection in 2012 while working on a research project on Depression-era quilt fabrics.[20] In his essay "Get Real! The Role of Objects in the Digital Age," Matthew MacArthur notes that "the first (and original) function of the museum is a place of research, complete with reference collections."[21] Polyvore, effectively, is a large visual reference collection for dress and textile studies. The only real difference is that its users, rather than passive visitors, are both its curators and the researchers hoping to make use of the collections.

We often think of the digital and life online as inherently ephemeral, but in a museum context, where exhibitions come and go with seasons, online content can actually provide a greater sense of longevity. It is comforting, in a way, to recognize that these curated collections' lives online long outpace the lifespan of the average museum exhibition. Permanent collection exhibits aside, had any of these collections been installed in a museum, they would have only lasted several weeks or months before they were taken down and replaced with something else.

While there are obviously numerous benefits of a user-curated social fashion site, there are pitfalls as well. One of the major drawbacks of Polyvore is that, at the end of the day, it *is* a shopping site. The individual objects within each collection display their basic metadata upon a mouse hover, which allows other users to discover not only the brand but also

Figure 3.2.   Polyvore collection: "The Byzantine Look." Created by the author.

the retail price of each object. Of course, in the museum world, the value of an object is somewhat carefully guarded and certainly never displayed to members of the public in an exhibition setting. Undoubtedly, many museum staff would be uncomfortable with this level of commercialization within the museum. I would argue, however, that many museums have effectively already gone commercial.

Tumblr

In contrast to Polyvore, which was initially intended as a retail-oriented enterprise and provides all of the available images for users via an algorithm, Tumblr[22] allows users to post their own images to visually oriented blogs. Tumblr is arguably an even more participatory platform than Polyvore (albeit one absolutely fraught with the potential for copyright issues). The bulk of the action on Tumblr is a kind of curatorial process that comes from an endless stream of liking (giving hearts) and "reblogging" others' image- and text-based posts. While Polyvore leverages users' existing brick-and-mortar world relationships, Tumblr is generally a place of anonymity, with users following blogs based on their pertinence to one's interests rather than through prior acquaintance.

This does not mean, however, that Tumblr is devoid of social interaction. On the contrary, the built-in mechanisms for providing feedback on the images chosen by others facilitate a steady stream of interaction. Joanna Turney, in her book *The Culture of Knitting*, noted:

> The main issue really is not whether it is possible to have "meaningful" relationships online, but to investigate the ways in which technology encourages new forms of sociability, which appear to succeed where traditional forms and rituals are increasingly seen to have failed. Anthropological approaches have investigated the ways in which virtual communities facilitate cultural reproduction, outlining how the Internet helps: "Communities and people come closer to a realization of who they already feel they 'really' are."[23]

Social sites like Tumblr not only constitute a new form of sociability but also facilitate cultural participation and reproduction. In her popular blog *Yarn Harlot*,[24] Stephanie Pearl-McPhee echoes this idea of a new sociability: "The Internet has fueled the socialization of knitters—it's great having an outlet where someone does want to talk to you about your new buttonhole technique or the beautifully hand-dyed merino you just got. It's become a huge knitting community—and while you might walk away from projects, you don't walk away from people, so the community continues to grow."[25] While there has been much research on the cultures of crafting communities, such as knitters and quiltmakers on social sites,[26] less material exists on the social historic dress community.

Perhaps even more than other social sites, Tumblr gets a bad rap for being frivolous and dominated by teenagers. And while there is a kernel of truth to this (in my forthcoming essay in *Hashtag Publics* I observe that "quilt and craft-related blogs, while quite abundant on Tumblr, are far outnumbered by Tumblr's golden quadrangle of food, humorous animals, sex, and fandom blogs"[27]), none of these uses of Tumblr are actually frivolous, nor is Tumblr entirely dominated by teenagers (and if it were, that would not be a bad thing). An example of an older (read: late twenties) user is Melissa, a twenty-eight-year-old from Pennsylvania who curates *Incense and Peppermints*, a blog dedicated to the fashion and music of the 1960s.[28] When I checked her blog in March 2015, she had recently reblogged a picture of iconic 1960s model Jean Shrimpton in some "natty knitwear."

Users with an interest in historic dress and textiles on Tumblr seem to be a motley crew of folks (mostly teenage and college age, but also older) interested in various fandoms, those with an interest in museums and the history of art generally, as well as designers and crafters looking for historical inspiration. Finding a possible commonality between these disparate users, Turney argued that "one might also suggest that a desire to become actively engaged in both blogging and knitting exemplifies a desire for a sense of touch, of engaging in and maintaining connections in the sensory and interpersonal wider world, contradicting [Howard] Rheingold's assertion that virtual communities are devoid of the sensory."[29] Besides this drive toward the sensory and the tangible, those with an interest in fashion and fabric, especially those who make some or all of their income through designing and marketing their own work, blog their creations on Tumblr as a form of entrepreneurship, building a fan base and a customer base.

Beyond that, however, there are several blogs that exist simply to serve as collections of disparate sources to inspire both the blog owner and others. *Fashion Illustration & Textiles*[30] and *Pattern Source*[31] are two good examples of this sort of curated blog. The anonymous owner of *Fashion Illustration & Textiles* says that their collection of fashion illustrations and textile designs "serves to inspire fellow artists, visionaries and fashion lovers by promoting up and coming artists & designers as well as masters in both fields."[32] In February 2015, designers featured on the blog included young and lesser-known designers such as Talula Christian[33] as well as the work of René Bouché, *Vogue* magazine illustrator from the 1930s to the 1960s. The juxtaposition of unknown and famous, new and old creates an interesting dialogue and sense of both continuity and change (something that museum curators generally aspire to do in their own curatorial work).

Many emerging designers simply share for empathy or encouragement: "These seams just aren't coming together!" Or they seek input from the community: "Does this color combination spoil the effect?" "Gold lamé, yay or nay?" Often times, though, designers share simply out of pride in finishing a project that they want others to see. Because fashion design and associated arts are such visual media (and this is even more the case online, where the tactile element is removed), designers in this area tend to favor media that privilege image over text, such as Instagram and Tumblr, though Facebook, of course, is still quite popular. On Tumblr in particular, there's a strong culture of sharing other's posts, so a designer who posts a photo of a project might get hundreds of random shares from people they do not even know.

A major difference between Polyvore and Tumblr is the means by which users can apply commentary (what we are calling the analog of the object label) to their chosen images. As on Twitter, Instagram, and other image-based social sites, Tumblr users provide commentary through the use of hashtags. Hashtags allow other users to search and find images and text-based posts as well as make observations or annotate, explain, or clarify the posted image. For those with an interest in historic dress, hashtags often refer to designers or periods, for example, #ysl (Yves Saint Laurent) or #1970s. Some tags, like #lesmoking (Le Smoking was a women's tuxedo created in 1966 by Yves Saint Laurent), are especially fun (and tricky) to search for, however, because for every one image of the actual Le Smoking tuxedo, one has to sort through at least one hundred pictures of various people smoking a cigarette. Fabrics like #leather and #vinyl, which can be used for a variety of applications other than vintage dress, can create a similar problem. #Vinyl, for example, usually returns results for posts about LPs rather than clothing made of vinyl. Ultimately, the fact that people are using the site for all sorts of topics and interests, not just fashion, makes documentation via tagging ultimately somewhat difficult.

For designers on Tumblr, however, the use of the hashtag remains the primary means of documenting work. Most designers will hashtag with their own name or the name of their label, such as #TalulaChristian. Designers and makers use tags for colors, fabrics, and patterns, for example, #chartreuse or #polka dot, as well as to indicate the general feel of the piece, such as #boho. Some users get a bit creative with hashtags (though this can make searching more difficult); instead of #boho, for example, one might use #outrageouslyboho. Hashtags can also reflect the dialect of the user's own family or community background (e.g., #bohoy'all) or their personal idiolect (e.g., #bohoisgenius).

All of these hashtags serve a dual purpose—they allow other users who might not follow the person who posted to find their pieces, and they allow the user who posted to organize their posts. Perhaps one of the most interesting things about how this nomenclature of tagging is evolving is that many of the most popular tags do not pertain to the object itself, but rather to the day on which it was posted, as in #museummonday or #throwbackthursday (sometimes simply expressed as #tbt), or the everyday changes that a designer faces, such as #designerproblems. Many of these tags are used on other social sites, such as Facebook, Twitter, and Instagram, as well.

#MuseumMonday at FIT

Related to the #museummonday hashtag is the practice of posting to Tumblr photographs of museum exhibitions taken by the user in the brick-and-mortar world. For example, in March 2015, one New Yorker's Tumblr blog, *Cirque du Fromage*[34] (which is fed by his Instagram account and also linked to his Twitter account), featured posts of several of his own photos of his visit to the Fashion Institute of Technology (FIT) Museum's exhibition *Yves Saint Laurent + Halston: Fashioning the 70s*.[35] Three photographs of the exhibition by the FIT Museum and posted to the museum's own Flickr Commons page are seen here (see figures 3.3–3.5). Rich and consistent use of tagging allows other users to follow along as he moves through the exhibition. One photograph, dominated by a shiny, gold leather jacket, was tagged as follows:

> #Luxe #yslhalston #yvessaintlaurent #halston #halstonettes #yvessaintlaurentrivegauche #fitmuseum #seventies #elsaperertti #chic #mesh #silk #cashmere #leather #gold #fashion #style #designer #fashionhistory.[36]

Another photo featured a display case containing three suede jackets and was tagged:

> #Ultrasuede #halston #yslhalston #museumatfit #fashion #minimal #american #designer #style #lizaminnelli #biancajagger #studio54 #pat-cleveland #halstonettes #jerryhall #ultrasuede.[37]

This particular user could have a future in authoring metadata schemes!

Analyzing user-applied hashtags and comparing them to those words used in the headings of museum exhibit labels or the hashtags used by the museum's own in-house social media campaign can be a very enlightening exercise for museum professionals. Patricia Mears and Emma McClendon organized the exhibition at FIT, and they used several keywords to denote thematic areas within the exhibition. These included "Menswear," "Exoticism," "Historicism," "Prints," "Evening," "Capes & Shimmer," and "Color." Intriguingly, this blogger seems to have eschewed these keywords in creating his own hashtags, focusing instead on particular colors and fabrics (which is a general convention of Tumblr, as it aids in searching) and personalities, such as Jerry Hall and Bianca Jagger. This interest in the cult of personality is also unsurprising, as Tumblr tends to be rich in fandoms and fan culture.

While one can explore this exhibition online on *Cirque du Fromage* (and undoubtedly on various other users' social media accounts as well), as with most contemporary museum exhibitions, the Fashion Institute of Technology Museum has its own rich social presence to accompany *Yves Saint Laurent + Halston*, including a blog and Twitter, Facebook, Pinterest,

Figure 3.3.   Halston Ultrasuede shirtdress, 1970s. *Yves Saint Laurent + Halston: Fashioning the 70s*. The Museum at FIT.

Figure 3.4. Halston and Yves Saint Laurent pajama sets, 1970s. *Yves Saint Laurent + Halston: Fashioning the 70s.* The Museum at FIT.

Figure 3.5. Halston evening ensemble in purple cashmere, 1970s. *Yves Saint Laurent + Halston: Fashioning the 70s*. The Museum at FIT.

and Flickr accounts. Noticeably absent here are Instagram and Tumblr, which tend to appeal to younger audiences. It is notable that the blogger used the FIT Museum's official hashtag for the exhibition, #yslhalston, even though the museum does not use the same social sites that he does. While a user might not appropriate a museum curator's nomenclature for their own hashtags, they will likely use the official hashtag.

As we have seen, digital photography and seamlessly integrated social sites allow people to curate their own worlds. Alongside the photographic record of this user's visit to the FIT Museum are a picture of the vodka cocktail he had in Brooklyn and a sign on a vending machine asking patrons to "please use quaters [sic]" only. Individuals infuse meaning into their surroundings, both in the brick-and-mortar world and online, based on their own attitudes and prior experiences. Even when one lives in an arguably exciting place, such as New York City, with its numerous cultural opportunities, one's numerous experiences there make the place feel downright quotidian. Sociologist Michel de Certeau has described this phenomenon as the "everydayness" of daily life.[38] Perhaps this level of personalization, this everydayness, feeds the stigma that these curated blogs do not have significance beyond the individual user.

I would argue, however, that the personalization makes one blogger's visit to the FIT a lot more interesting than it would be without juxtaposition of the seemingly incongruous slices of his life. So many museum exhibitions feel cold or alienating to the visitor because the curator is a disembodied voice with no apparent personality. Even a user who may not be interested in Yves Saint Laurent or Halston might be more inclined to pay attention when that material is presented by an everyday person in the context of their unique sense of humor and the trappings of their daily life.

User-Curation, Museums, and the Participatory Web

For a variety of reasons, some museum professionals are still loath to relinquish their curatorial authority to the public, this vodka-swilling, museum-visiting rabble. Notions of the expert (and that one needs an advanced degree to be one) and professionalism still prevent a major sea change in curatorial practice. In her essay in *Letting Go? Sharing Historical Authority in a User-Generated World*, Kathleen McLean notes that "museums, conceived and perceived as sites of authority, still embody the 'information transmission' model of learning that developed in the late 1800s, with museums as the source of expert knowledge and the visitors as recipients of that expertise."[39] The idea that it is okay, and even highly desirable, for historians to let go of some of their traditional curatorial authority is, for some, a bitter pill to swallow.

These examples of curated collections on Polyvore and curated blogs on Tumblr, however, point to a shift that *is* occurring in museum practice and public history. Whether high tech or low tech, the ways in which we use technology are shifting the role of authority from being vested in a historical cultural domain, such as the museum or the university history department, to a community or user-generated body of information that is critiqued within the community. In a 2011 blog post, Smithsonian social media manager Elissa Frankle wrote, "In the history museum of the future, curators' work will be driven by our audiences' curiosity, and their preference for inquiry over certainty."[40] Sharing of historical authority with diverse publics and embracing new technologies that can facilitate such sharing will arguably be one of the main value shifts in museum work in the twenty-first century. This sharing will largely (and has already begun to) occur on the participatory Web.

Public Curation and the Participatory Web

How does the participatory Web work? Users do something that generates information (they upload content, rate things, comment, buy things, or click search results), and the system adapts responsively to those participatory actions, providing customized experiences based on user behavior. Nina Simon, museum blogger,[41] executive director of the Santa Cruz Museum of Art & History, and author of *The Participatory Museum*,[42] is one of the preeminent proponents of visitor and community participation in museums. Taking ideas about arts participation (mostly from the world of museums and other cultural nonprofits) and participatory culture (mostly from the digital world), she defines a participatory museum as one that displays objects created by visitors, generates maps of most popular or provocative exhibits based on visitors' comments, helps visitors find other people (staff or visitors) with shared interests with whom to engage in content-specific activities or discussions, and provides a public forum for visitors and staff members to ask and answer each other's questions.

Public curation is democratic and inclusive. Not only is participatory design more engaging for the visitor, but it is also beneficial for the visitor *and* the institution. Museum studies scholar Eileen Hooper-Greenhill envisions a Post-Museum, "a site of mutual understanding, where knowledge is constructed, rather than transmitted, through the account of multiple subjectivities and identities."[43] Rather than the monotone of the museum curator's perspective, user-generated content such as public curation as seen on Polyvore and Tumblr allows for the presentation of multiple perspectives and worldviews from the public to the public.

This notion of public curation as a form of many-to-many communication is not a new one. Indeed, playwright Bertolt Brecht, a contemporary to the popularization of radio (and a period of great transition in arts participation), wrote in his essay "Radio as a Means of Communication" (1932) that radio need not be merely a means for distribution of information and culture from one individual source to the masses. This prophetic piece proposes an alternate future for radio in which people both create and receive content rather than simply taking in content from a few sources out of their control. Anticipating the Internet by about sixty years, Brecht argued that technology need not determine the function and use of radio, that people could instead use radio for two-way broadcasting, not unlike "Broadcast it yourself," the slogan of user-generated video site YouTube.

> Nor does radio, in my opinion, suffice as a method of making the home cozy and family life possible again so we can cheerfully leave aside the question whether what it cannot achieve is in any case desirable. But quite apart from its dubious function (to offer a lot is to offer no one anything), radio is one-sided when it should have two sides. It is a pure instrument of distribution: it merely hands things out. And now to be positive, that is to say, to turn to the positive side of radio, here is a proposal to give radio a new function: Radio should be converted from a distribution system to a communication system. Radio could be the most wonderful public communication system imaginable, a gigantic system of channels—could be, that is, if it were capable not only of transmitting but of receiving, of making the listener not only hear but also speak, not of isolating him but of connecting him. This means that radio would have to give up being a purveyor and organise the listener as purveyor.[44]

In an ideal world, the individual, not some centralized source, is the purveyor of culture. The ethos of the folk is the ethos of the social Web.

User-Curation as Arts Participation

"The characteristic spirit, prevalent tone of sentiment, of a people or community; the 'genius' of an institution or system." This is how *ethos* is defined, according to the *Oxford English Dictionary*.[45] Ethos is key to understanding why it is that students of fashion history from a variety of walks of life have come to not only use but also embrace and rely upon social sites such as Polyvore. Key to the social Web's ethos is a value of community.

This is in direct contrast to the archetypal *artist* in the Western tradition, which glorifies the cult of the individual.

The ethos of the social Web, with its emphasis on the power of online communities and social networks, its value on the collective knowledge of the group (as with the masses-edited *Wikipedia*) rather than the knowledge of any one expert individual, is very much the folk art ethos. Far from strange bedfellows, artists, designers, crafters, and the champions of the social Web—bloggers, wiki editors, and the like—have the same base goals and values: to foster a community of makers, a participatory culture of meaning and meaning-making reminiscent of the nineteenth-century days of quilting bees and front porch family sings.

Participatory culture can be defined as culture in which there are low barriers to artistic and civic engagement.[46] What does the motto of the National Endowment for the Arts, "A great nation deserves great art," mean in this context? Is a log cabin quilt "great art"? Is *Downton Abbey* fan fiction? Is a handmade duck decoy, or a berry basket? Is the clothing I design for my avatar? "Great art" is hardly participatory culture.

Sousa, the Songs of the Day, and the Old Songs

Legal scholar Lawrence Lessig is a champion of revealing sometimes-antiquated legal opinions on intellectual property and rights management and how those opinions influence behavior online. As we saw in the examples from Polyvore and Tumblr, key to contemporary life (and law) online is the notion of participatory culture. Lessig has described participatory culture and consumer culture as read-write and read-only cultures, respectively (these terms referring to the levels of permission required for content creation in word processing and other computer programs). For Lessig, read-write culture, the ability to create as well as consume the culture around us, is a cultural right, a right that is constantly under fire from not only broadcasters of read-only culture but also the American legal system itself. A decline in participatory culture in music (a decline in listen-sing culture, if you will), precipitated by the adoption of new recording and playback technologies, similarly troubled John Philip Sousa a century ago. In 1906, Sousa testified before the Congress of the United States, saying, "These Talking Machines [gramophones] are going to ruin artistic development of music in this country. When I was a boy, in front of every house in the summer evenings you would find young people together singing the songs of the day, or the old songs. Today you hear these infernal machines going night and day. We will not have a vocal cord left."[47] Sousa's remarks were, in hindsight, quite prescient. The early twentieth century was a period of great flux in American arts participation.

In the nineteenth century, engagement meant playing the piano or acting in a home theatrical.

> Through much of the nineteenth century, the piano had served as the nation's archetypal cultural hearth, and images of a family sing or an informal after-dinner performance of a classical piece by a young student were staples of American domesticity. Then, the ability to sing or play music and, for that matter, drawing and the writing and recitation of poetry were considered everyday skills, integrated into family life as thoroughly as sewing or the canning of autumn garden produce.[48]

In the twentieth century, however, engagement in the arts meant passive viewing and enjoyment of the "high arts" in a nonprofit setting. One could argue that, rather than Americans ceasing to engage with arts, the very definition of what it means to be engaged changed instead. The nineteenth-century definition of arts engagement in America—sewing, quilting, drawing, homemade music, and after-dinner theatricals—simply was not the twentieth-century definition of participatory culture. In his introduction to *Engaging Art*, Bill Ivey, folklorist and former director of the National Endowment for the Arts, noted that 1909 was the "high water mark" for piano sales in America.[49]

Steven Tepper and Bill Ivey's collection *Engaging Art* proposes multiple historically dependent definitions for participation in the arts, and traces the history of arts engagement in America from a truly participatory engagement in the nineteenth century (piano playing, other kinds of homemade music, home theatricals, etc.) to a passive engagement in the twentieth century as arts appreciation, or to put it bluntly, arts consumption of viewing paintings in galleries, listening to concerts in performing arts centers, and so on, and now back to a more active engagement online in the twenty-first century with blogging and photosharing sites such as Instagram. The essays in this collection very clearly show how arts participation is shaped by technology—television, radio, film, and home listening and viewing formats—and commerce, and why arts participation is so important. Ultimately, technology and commerce shape participation in the arts. The three major broadcast technologies of the early twentieth century—film, radio, and television—do not require much participation from the public that consumes them, other than looking or listening over time. These top-down, read-only technologies allowed for easy marketing to consumers in a capitalist society and easy control of the political and cultural information available to the masses.

A Theory of Arts Participation

A theory of arts participation proposed by arts researcher Alan Brown offers one means by which to understand the binary of read-write and read-only culture in terms of arts participation. Brown suggests a hierarchy of five modes of arts participation: ambient, observational, curatorial, interpretive, and inventive.[50] Ambient participation refers to unplanned arts experiences, such as happening upon a folk festival while walking downtown, whereas, slightly higher up the scale, observational participation includes planned arts attendance, such as attending the ballet or visiting a museum. Curatorial participation involves selecting and arranging works. This is a midlevel form of participation and describes the user-curated collections on Polyvore as well as the (re)blogging activity on Tumblr to be seen later in this chapter. Interpretive participation refers to performance of a preexisting piece, such as a home theatrical of a published play or singing or playing an existing song. Finally, atop the hierarchy of arts participation is inventive participation, which involves the creation of original works of visual art, music, dance, and theater in various media and genres.

The ways in which people consumed these new technologies—photography, film, radio, and television—changed the very notion of what it meant to participate in the arts. Appreciation and consumption, *not performance or invention or curation*, became the dominant form of arts participation in the United States in the twentieth century.

The Problem of Technological Determinism

I must be careful here, before continuing, to point out that though I argue that technology shapes arts participation, my view is far from technological determinism. Technological determinism fundamentally deals with causality. A technological determinist would argue that technologies, rather than social or cultural shifts, drive history. In his book *Television, Technology and Cultural Form*, Raymond Williams wrote of the dangers of such a view of history. Williams argued that rather than looking at effects (what social and cultural phenomena television may have led to), one should look at the causes of television—what social and cultural phenomena brought television into existence. This is very against the rhetoric of technological determinism.

If television itself was the cause of social ills such as youth violence and rampant consumerism, then society could simply seek to modify its effects, but since the television is in fact a product of social forces, as opposed to a cause, we must seek the causes of television (or video games or Internet media or any other technological form) within culture. While some social, religious, civic, and political leaders worry over the effects of television—sex, violence, political manipulation, cultural degradation, and the like—these things are happening much more broadly in Western culture within the mass media. In essence, the determinist view is that if television (or any other technological form) had not been invented, then social change would never have occurred. A purely deterministic view belies the fact that technologies such as television, radio, the Internet, and the automobile could have developed completely differently had other social, cultural, political, and economic forces been at work. Rather than driving history, technological change, as noted by Carolyn Marvin in *When Old Technologies Were New: Thinking about Electronic Communication in the Nineteenth Century*, actually upholds social and cultural norms. Technologies, and the changes that they effect, are put into motion not by some pseudo-natural force of innovation but instead by the shifting social norms and expectations that make those new technologies desirable.

Arts Participation beyond the High Arts
As evidenced by the Survey of Public Participation in the Arts (SPPA), a survey of public arts participation in the United States conducted every five years by the National Endowment for the Arts, arts organizations have largely focused on the centralized sources of culture rather than individual creators of culture.[51] The survey focuses on participation as attendance at cultural nonprofits—museums, orchestras, ballets, theaters, and the like—rather than noninstitutionalized grassroots efforts or lone individuals actively engaged in arts participation. When the survey first began in the 1970s, the SPPA may have been a fairly accurate barometer of arts participation (as it was then defined). Today, however, the idea of attendance at cultural nonprofits as the sole or even most important metric of arts participation is no longer an accurate measure in the early twenty-first century. With new digital tools on the Web, individuals can create everything from original music videos to digital quilts. The social Web has impacted not only the means of production of culture, allowing for more active participation in the creation of culture on the part of individuals, but also the means of distribution. New media scholar Henry Jenkins has noted that social technologies online enable unique new channels for the distribution of amateur artistic content, as well as new means by which to

measure participation, including the number of hits to a webpage and the like.[52] Ironically, it was technology that, in the early twentieth century, led to the decline of folk culture and the rise of a top-down mass broadcast culture.

> Much of it [folk culture on the Web] can be produced and consumed in the home; many people contribute and learn from each other (without necessarily considering themselves professional artists); and much of what gets produced is considered community property. From this vantage point, the next great transformation of America's cultural life feels more like a return to an earlier era of participatory culture rather than the onset of some new, unfamiliar form of postmodern cyberculture.[53]

Far from an "unfamiliar form of postmodern cyberculture," folk participation in the arts and culture on the Web is, one could argue, a more authentically American cultural form than that surveyed by the SPPA.

Tocqueville, in *Democracy in America*, noted that, unlike any country in Europe, in America, people naturally formed and participated in organizations of all kinds: religious, political, cultural. Indeed, in *Engaging Art*, Ivey and Tepper describe a positive link between participation in the arts and culture and political participation. For a more active and engaged society, America needs participation in the arts. Ivey has advocated a cultural voucher system in which citizens receive a voucher that pays for participation in museums and other arts and cultural events. This is one possible solution. The creation of a cabinet-level secretary of the arts or a multiagency White House office (structurally similar to the Office of National Security) would also be steps in the right direction.

Civic participation is strongly correlated with arts and cultural participation.[54] Thus, participation in the arts is integral to maintaining a creative and productive citizenry that can compete on the world market and world stage in the decades to come. In their analysis of demographic correlates to traditional cultural participation in the United States, Tepper and Gao note that young people, the future of any society, have historically been left out of the arts.[55] New forms of cultural participation online have already done much to change this; in fact, young people are at the forefront of much of the content creation on the Web today.[56] Today, art is much more likely to be actively integrated into young people's daily lives—such as curating collections of historic dress on a social website—rather than a one-time event, such as a field trip or an evening at the opera with their parents. And it is not a bad thing that the next generation of digital natives is more likely to be engaged in the arts by creating a mashup than attending the opera.

Appreciation of the arts, of course, does not apply only to the "high arts." The (re)emergence of a do-it-yourself aesthetic online should ultimately be seen as a revival of folk culture. As I have already noted, just as it was at the turn of the last century with the rise of radio, film, and the phonograph, arts and cultural participation is again in a state of transition. Folk art, from quilting bees to contra dances, is inherently participatory, and it is the folk arts, such as quilting, that kept truly participatory culture alive through the twentieth century, and now, in the twenty-first century, artists, designers, crafters, and curators are in the vanguard of cultural participation on the Web, from Instagrammed photographs to curated collections to blogs.

In her sourcebook on African American quilting, *Black Threads*, Kyra Hicks published a study on how African American quiltmakers were using the Internet (2003).[57] She found that African American quiltmakers were using the Web for quilt-related e-mails, quilt auctions, online fabric shopping, pattern swaps, and round robins, sharing images of their own quilts with others, research on contemporary and historic quilts, and many other applications. Hicks noted that many of these activities have allowed for the creation of close-knit communities of African American quiltmakers online. The results of Hicks's research are echoed in the literary criticism of Elaine Showalter. In discussing Alice Walker's "Everyday Use," Showalter wrote, "Virginia Woolf's image of a room of one's own, so enabling for women modernists in England seeking privacy and autonomy, seems somehow isolated and remote for American women writers, especially black writers, today."[58] While the potential is there for the computer and the Web to be socially isolating, for many American women artists today—writers and quiltmakers alike—collaboration, community, and collective knowledge are at the heart of the creative process. Web technologies could (in the technologically deterministic view) have created an uneasy social isolation, an unwilling imprisonment in a room of one's own. Instead, communities of women (and men) online have used the social Web to make connections with those with common interests, build social networks, and share artistic and cultural knowledge.

Little Communities and Collective Knowledge
In *The Little Community: Viewpoints for the Study of a Human Whole*, Robert Redfield defines "the little community" as a small, distinctive, homogenous, and self-sufficient organization of people.[59] Aficionados of vintage fashion or a particular craft such as knitting and quiltmaking do indeed

form small, distinctive, homogenous, and self-sufficient organizations of people within the much larger human community online. The "little community" of vintage couture lovers on Polyvore, for example, exhibits many attributes of small communities as described by Redfield. As a community, they function within specific human ecological systems. Within these ecological systems, social structures and social norms have developed, such as the types of comments posted on a wall or the frequency of posting by certain users. The vintage fashion community on Polyvore has a history, or rather histories, and a fairly coherent ethos, or outlook on life. There are also communities within the "little community" of vintage fashion on Polyvore, such as fans of specific models or celebrities, and those with common interests that most appeal to a part rather than the whole of the group, such as African American fashion.

User-curated histories of dress on the social Web may also be understood in the context of what cybertheorist Pierre Lévy termed "collective intelligence." In his theoretical work, *Cyberculture*, Lévy describes the collective intelligence brought about by online communication in this way.

> My hypothesis is that cyberculture reinstates the copresence of messages and their context, which had been the current of oral societies, but on a different scale and on a different plane. The new universality no longer depends on self-sufficient texts, on the fixity and independence of signification. It is constructed and extended by interconnecting messages with one another, by their continuous ramification through virtual communities, which instills in them varied meanings that are continuously renewed.[60]

In laymen's terms, one can understand the collective intelligence of the social Web in this way: No one user knows everything, not even everything about their favorite vintage fashion icon, and every user actively creating content has something slightly different to offer the community. All of the content uploaded amounts to the collective intelligence of the vintage fashion community, a body of knowledge that no one user can ever know in its entirety, for it is simply too vast. But, collectively, individual people, many of them still students, are creating a massive, fairly cohesive body of knowledge online.

Sousa, Remixed

To return to the example of Sousa, the singing of "the songs of the day and the old songs" can be read as a historical antecedent to user-generated videos, mashups, and other content that people, especially young people, are creating online today. In his 2007 TED Talk on "Laws That Choke Creativity," legal scholar Lawrence Lessig argued:

> Digital technology is the opportunity for the revival of these vocal cords that he spoke so passionately about. User-generated content, celebrating amateur culture. By which I don't mean amateurish culture, I mean culture where people produce for the love of what they're doing and not for the money. I mean the culture that your kids are producing all the time. For when you think of what Sousa romanticized in the young people together, singing the songs of the day, or the old songs, you should recognize what your kids are doing now. Taking the songs of the day and the old songs and remixing them to make something different. It's how they understand access to this culture.[61]

To value participatory culture—including participation in the arts—is to value amateur, grassroots culture. "The world of Web 2.0 is also the world of what Dan Gillmor calls 'we, the media,' a world in which 'the former audience,' not a few people in a back room, decides what's important."[62] Technology, and specifically the social Web, has the power to connect with and be relevant to various communities, encouraging the public to actively participate in real-time content curation and other cultural activities.

Online collections allow a variety of cultural institutions to reach rural audiences who previously did not have such access, both in the United States and around the world. Social sites online allow cultural organizations to build communities online and connect with a large population, especially people under twenty-five, who might not become engaged without this new kind of Web presence. Social media also shifts the role of authority from being vested in a historical cultural domain, such as the museum, to a community or user-generated body of information that is critiqued within the community.

To use another example from before the rise of the culture industry, the young women in Louisa May Alcott's *Little Women*—Meg, Jo, Beth, and Amy March—did not watch a DVD or made-for-TV movie production of *Pilgrim's Progress*. With their home as the backdrop of Bunyan's work, they put on the production of *Pilgrim's Progress* themselves, acting rather than watching. "Do you remember how you used to play *Pilgrim's Progress* when you were little things? Nothing delighted you more than to have me tie my piece-bags on your back for burdens, give you hats and sticks and rolls of paper, and let you travel through the house from the cellar, which was the City of Destruction, up, up, to the housetop, where you had all the lovely things you could collect in the Celestial City."[63] Of course, the video and communications technologies that make television and DVDs possible did not exist in the nineteenth century. During the 1800s, for the March sisters to enjoy a production of *Pilgrim's Progress*, they had to put it on themselves as a home theatrical. Home theatricals fell from favor in the twentieth century, as people consumed radio, film, and television productions. Folk life and homemade culture ebbed as mainstream, top-down, broadcast culture flourished. However, this is not the whole story in the early twenty-first century. Social technologies are a critical element for the revitalization of grassroots culture, of the handmade. It is of tremendous significance that the content to be found relating to quilting on these kinds of social applications has been generated by (young) enthusiasts of fashion history to build the collective knowledge of the online vintage couture community. In the early twenty-first century, users within the community, rather than retail corporations (though Polyvore is a gray area here) or Internet news media, drive content on the social Web.

One concrete example of a professionally curated project prioritizing user-generated content is Learning to Love You More. Created by independent filmmaker Miranda July (*Me and You and Everyone We Know*), the website ran from 2002 to 2010 and featured over eight thousand user submissions to crowdsourced assignments proposed by July. The very first assignment for the project (out of seventy) asked the public to make a child's outfit in an adult size,[64] photograph it, and upload it to the site. Most of the submissions—there were seventeen in total—were a variation on the romper.[65] While the public responses to these assignment constitute invention—the highest form of arts participation on Alan Brown's scale—one could argue that the curation on Polyvore and Tumblr is ultimately more interesting from a museum learning perspective because works curated on Polyvore and Tumblr (or content posted to other social sites) are not prompted or provoked by an outside authority but rather spontaneously uploaded.

Like many crowdsourced projects (as well as social media sites), Learning to Love You More lived online. User-generated content is quite compelling when brought into the physical space of the museum, however. In his essay "Curating New Media," Matthew Gansallo explores how (and how not) to bring media into the museum, asking, "How can an environment of ongoing process and human interaction, which has been at the core of the development of artistic projects related to the Internet, be represented and presented in the museum project?"[66] Surely there is a better solution for display of and interaction with social sites and other user-generated content than a computer workstation or a tablet on a bungee cord set up in the corner of the museum gallery. User-curation is one possible solution to this quandary.

The Six-Point Manifesto

As we have seen, this digital shift in participatory culture, back to a read-write culture, creates new opportunities and models for change for museums (as well as challenges for the more conservative element within the museum, the academy, policymakers, and the legal community). Here are six tenets of user-curation that museum staff members could (and should) make a part of the conversation as they seek to make their institutions more participatory:

Tenets of User-Curation

1. User-curation is an excellent model for museum learning, as it is intrinsically motivated and gives users a sense of power and agency.
2. User-curated collections are quite personal, reflecting the user's own style and sense of self. Even though user-curation is often highly personalized, this individualization tends to have universal rather than particular appeal.
3. User-curators have a right to their own language. They should feel free to create their own hashtags and nomenclature rather than appropriating those in use at the museum.
4. Museums should celebrate amateur culture and actively encourage, rather than condemn, users' noncommercial online curation of their objects.
5. The system of arts patronage in the United States should be changed so that amateur designers and curators are on a more equal footing with the professionals.
6. Museums and other cultural nonprofits should prioritize the creation and display of user-generated content.

The curatorial work, undertaken on a free and spontaneous basis, by thousands of (young) people in online social sites such as Polyvore and Tumblr provides answers—or at least a way forward—for museums seeking to engage audiences in the curatorial process. One question remains thoroughly unanswered, however: Is there still a place for curatorial authority in the world of the participatory museum?

A Need for Historical Authority?

Perhaps a veteran curator, even after reading this chapter, might think that this reblogging of images on Tumblr or curation of fashion on Polyvore is rather unimportant for the historian. Well, in a sense, that's true. Much of the content reblogged on Tumblr, while pretty or funny or momentarily interesting, is at the end of the day thoroughly unremarkable. But this archiving of the unremarkable is precisely what I find so fascinating here. Everyday people, through user-generated content, choose to archive images of objects important to them, not museum curators or historians. And, while perhaps unremarkable now, if these Tumblr blogs and Polyvore collections were to be archived properly, this digital participatory culture would, I think, be of tremendous value to the dress and textile historians of the future.

As we have seen in this chapter, new, visual, and object-related social platforms, such as Polyvore and Tumblr, can enable apparel and craft communities online to self-fashion their unique body of collective knowledge. Most fashion bloggers and designers see sharing online as a social and community building activity, but the reality is that, consciously or not, by putting this stuff online, they are creating a vast, rich historical record, albeit one that's going to be a real pain for future scholars to work through and catalog. One of the key jobs of the twenty-first-century historian will be to organize and interpret digital collections for the public. Tumblr, Polyvore, Instagram, Twitter—none of these come with object labels, let alone a finding aid.

Notes

1. Susan Sontag, quoted in *The Cheap Date Guide to Style*, Kira Jolliffe and Bay Garnett (New York: Universe Publishing, 2008), 8.

2. Coco Mault, "Audrey Hepburn on the Moon," Flickr Commons, https://www.flickr.com/photos/contusion/7485321088/in/photolist-cpseb9.

3. Polyvore.com.

4. Phyllis Tortora and Keith Eubank, *Survey of Historic Costume*, 3rd ed. (New York: Fairchild, 1998), 460–63.

5. Foxboro, "Swinging London," Polyvore, http://www.polyvore.com/swinging_london/set?id=24909796&lid=648523.

6. Foxboro, "Twiggy," Polyvore, http://www.polyvore.com/twiggy/set?id=24619170&lid=648523.

7. Lilysue, "Donyale Luna," Polyvore, http://www.polyvore.com/donyale_luna/set?id=118430976.

8. AlexD, "Donyale Luna," Polyvore, http://www.polyvore.com/donyale_luna/set?id=149298530.

9. AlexD, "Alex Dyer," Polyvore, http://alexd.polyvore.com.

10. Vlg-Budde, "Marianne Faithfull inspired," Polyvore, http://www.polyvore.com/marianne_faithfull_inspired/set?id=112861415.

11. Vlg-Budde.

12. Timothy Ambrose and Crispin Paine, *Museum Basics*, 3rd ed. (London: Routledge, 2012), 149.

13. Ambrose and Paine, 149.

14. Bohemians, "Style Inspiration: Anita Pallenberg," Polyvore, http://www.polyvore.com/style_inspiration_anita_pallenberg/set?id=73731085.

15. Bohemians.

16. Anita Pallenberg, quoted in Jolliffe and Garnett, 122.

17. John H. Falk and Lynn D. Dierking, *Learning from Museums: Visitor Experiences and the Making of Meaning* (Walnut Creek, CA: Alta Mira Press, 2000).

18. Jolliffe and Garnett, 9.

19. Falk and Dierking, 21.

20. Amanda Sikarskie, "Social Media for Quilt History," American Quilt Study Group, Lincoln, NE, October 6, 2012.

21. Matthew MacArthur, "Get Real! The Role of Objects in the Digital Age," in *Letting Go? Sharing Historical Authority in a User-Generated World*, eds. Bill Adair, Benjamin Filene, and Laura Koloski (Philadelphia: Pew Center for Arts and Heritage, 2011), 57.

22. Tumblr.com.

23. Joanna Turney, *The Culture of Knitting* (Oxford: Berg, 2009), 151.

24. Stephanie Pearl-McPhee, *Yarn Harlot*, http://www.yarnharlot.ca/.

25. Quoted in Turney, 151.

26. See the bibliography of my dissertation, "Fiberspace" (Michigan State University, 2011).

27. Amanda Sikarskie, "Living the #Quilt Life: Talking about Quiltmaking on Tumblr," in *Hashtag Publics*, ed. Nathan Rambukkana (New York: Peter Lang, 2015).

28. Melissa, *Incense and Peppermints*, Tumblr, http://thewonderfulworldofthe60s.tumblr.com/.

29. Turney, 151.

30. *Fashion Illustration & Textiles*, Tumblr, http://fashionillustration-textiles.tumblr.com/.

31. *Pattern Source*, Tumblr, http://patternsource.tumblr.com/.

32. *Fashion Illustration & Textiles*.

33. Talula Christian, *Talula Christian*, Tumblr, http://talulachristian.tumblr.com/.

34. Michael Cunningham, *Cirque du Fromage*, http://www.cirquedufromage.com/.

35. The online exhibition for *Yves Saint Laurent + Halston: Fashioning the 70s* is available at http://exhibitions.fitnyc.edu/ysl-halston/.

36. Michael Cunningham, https://instagram.com/p/0LVwRSPk5o/.

37. Michael Cunningham, https://instagram.com/p/0LUyzRPk3i/.

38. Michel de Certeau, quoted in Konstantinos Arvanitis, "Museums Outside Walls: Mobile Phones and the Museum in the Everyday," in *Museums in a Digital Age*, ed. Ross Parry (London: Routledge, 2010), 172.

39. Kathleen McLean, "Whose Questions, Whose Conversations?" in *Letting Go? Sharing Historical Authority in a User-Generated World*, eds. Bill Adair, Benjamin Filene, and Laura Koloski (Philadelphia: Pew Center for Arts and Heritage, 2011), 70.

40. Elissa Frankle, "More Crowdsourced Scholarship: Citizen History," *Center for the Future of Museums Blog*, July 28, 2011, http://futureofmuseums.blogspot.com/2011/07/more-crowdsourced-scholarship-citizen.html.

41. Nina Simon, *Museum 2.0*, http://museumtwo.blogspot.com.

42. Nina Simon, *The Participatory Museum* (Santa Cruz, CA: Museum 2.0, 2010).

43. Eileen Hooper-Greenhill, quoted in Arvanitis, 171.

44. Bertolt Brecht, "Radio as a Means of Communication: A Talk on the Function of Radio," http://www.nyklewicz.com/brecht.html.

45. "Ethos," *Oxford English Dictionary*, http://www.oed.com/viewdictionary entry/Entry/64840.

46. Steven Tepper and Bill Ivey, eds., *Engaging Art: The Next Great Transformation of America's Cultural Life* (London: Routledge, 2008), 174.

47. Lawrence Lessig, "Laws that Choke Creativity," TED Talks (March 2007), https://www.ted.com/talks/larry_lessig_says_the_law_is_strangling_creativity.

48. Bill Ivey, *Arts, Inc.: How Greed and Neglect Have Destroyed Our Cultural Rights* (Berkeley and Los Angeles: University of California Press, 2008), 3.

49. Tepper and Ivey, 3.

50. Tepper and Ivey, 35–36.

51. Tepper and Ivey, 1.

52. Tepper and Ivey, 370.

53. Tepper and Ivey, 371.

54. Steven Tepper and Yang Gao, "Engaging Art: What Counts?" in *Engaging Art: The Next Great Transformation of America's Cultural Life*, eds. Steven Tepper and Bill Ivey (London: Routledge, 2008), 19.

55. Tepper and Gao, 29–30.

56. Pew Internet.

57. Kyra Hicks, *Black Threads: An African American Quilting Sourcebook* (Jefferson, NC: McFarland, 2003).

58. Elaine Showalter, "Common Threads," in *Sister's Choice: Tradition and Change in American Women's Writing* (New York: Oxford University Press, 1991), 175.

59. Robert Redfield, *The Little Community: Viewpoints for the Study of a Human Whole* (Chicago: University of Chicago Press, 1958), 4.

60. Pierre Lévy, *Cyberculture* (Minneapolis: University of Minnesota Press, 2001), xiv.

61. Lessig, "Laws That Choke Creativity."

62. Tim O'Reilly, "What Is Web 2.0?" *O'Reilly Media*, http://oreilly.com/web2/archive/what-is-web-20.html.

63. Louisa May Alcott, *Little Women* (New York: Dutton, 1948), 14.

64. Miranda July, "Make a Child's Outfit in an Adult Size," Learning to Love You More, http://www.learningtoloveyoumore.com/reports/1/1.php.

65. Wheat Wurtzburger and Anna Kerlin, "Child's Outfit in an Adult Size," Learning to Love You More, http://www.learningtoloveyoumore.com/reports/1/wurtzburger_wheat.php.

66. Matthew Gansallo, "Curating New Media," in *Museums in a Digital Age*, ed. Ross Parry (London: Routledge, 2010), 344.

Interpretation   **4**

THIS CHAPTER TAKES US FROM CURATION TO INTERPRETATION—and to the more positive side of the academic historian as curatorial authority. We saw in chapter 3 that everyday people do a remarkable job at curating their own collections of material objects online, and even of introducing others to the objects' histories. Indeed, many people, including historiographer Keith Jenkins, now question the very relevance of the professional historian.

> In his polemic *Refiguring History*, Keith Jenkins portrays professional historians as labouring under illusions and clinging to self-definitions which are foolish and predicated upon falsehoods. He argues that historians access the past by deploying a particular set of "discursive skills" yet that they are as expert in the studying of "the before now" as "anyone": "journalists, politicians, media commentators, film makers, artists—can and do successfully access 'the before now' often in ingenious ways which pay scant regard for the 'skills and methods' of the historian."[1]

I was recently struck by this notion of artists accessing past, or the "before now," as Jenkins calls it, when I heard about the Rolling Stones' new historical exhibition, cheekily titled *Exhibitionism*.[2] Largely curated by Mick Jagger and drummer Charlie Watts, and featuring costumes, instruments, and photographs from the four members' own personal collections, the exhibition looks very much indeed like it will "pay scant regard for the 'skills and methods' of the historian."

If artists are bypassing historians and curating their own traveling exhibitions of their own work and lives, where, then, does that leave the historian? Cultural historian Jerome de Groot notes that Jenkins's roasting of professional historians raises key questions about the nature of history and who can (and should) interpret history for the public. He asks, "If 'the past' is after all an empty signifier, just what are the semiotic processes involved in constructing, perpetuating and consuming meaning—what strategies are in place for pouring sense into such representational aporia?"[3] Is anyone really equally capable of accessing the past as a trained historian? Well, yes, actually, provided, of course, that "anyone" is a keen and careful researcher and a good storyteller.

De Groot notes that what prompted him to write *Consuming History* was the fact that two key transformations in the ways in which the public relates to history had gone largely unremarked upon by academic historians and museums. "The first was a shift in access [of the sort discussed at length in chapters 2 and 3 of this book]—from reality TV to new curatorial practice to popular history books to Web 2.0—that allowed the individual to seemingly conceptually and materially circumvent the historical professional and appear to engage with the 'past' in a more direct fashion."[4] Stepping aside and watching the public curate their own collections and fashion their own historical narratives is not, as discussed in chapter 3, necessarily a bad thing. In fact, it can be quite a good thing. But problems can arise in relation to the second transformation that de Groot discerned: "Second, and concurrently (and somewhat contradictorily), History was increasingly prevalent as a cultural, social and economic trope and genre."[5] That is, now more than ever history is for most people a commodity to be packaged, sold, and consumed. We see this in the plethora of very commercially oriented history-related programming that has emerged on cable television in recent years—with the public interest in historical objects primarily lying in their economic potential—goods that can be pawned or auctioned, bought or sold. We see this online as well. Polyvore, for example, the social site with so much potential for users to curate their own histories of dress, is, at its core, a shopping site.

What exactly are historians and museum curators good for then? The answer, I think, lies in the unique set of discursive skills possessed by historians. Unlike both Polyvore users with a passion for curation and venerable rock bands who have decided to try their hand at curating an exhibition, professional historians are trained in *interpretation*. That is, to use Jerome de Groot's idea of popular understanding of the past as a series of semiotic processes,[6] in constructing and perpetuating meaning and in packaging meaning for consumption. I had the chance to work on a major interpretive project in 2013, when I created interpretive materials for the instructional needlework program *Erica*, a PBS series from the 1970s starring British embroidery guru Erica Wilson, for the WGBH Boston Media

Library and Archives as part of a larger digitization project. In the course of this chapter of *Textile Collections,* I will use the interpretation of the Erica Wilson show for a new, online audience as a core example as I demonstrate these three key steps in historical interpretation in three sections: "Constructing Meaning: Interpreting *Erica,*" "Perpetuating Meaning: Postmodernism's Victorian Afterlife," and "Consuming Meaning: Shopping for History Online." The chapter concludes with a final admonition not to become a tweed-clad "Rip Van Recluse."

Constructing Meaning: Interpreting *Erica*

Now that we have determined that there is indeed still a place for professional historians in a user-driven world, let us turn for a moment to the concept of interpretation. To interpret simply means to make explicable. Its core meaning is linguistic; for example, if I attempt to order from a menu in a Parisian street café but do not know what "escargot" means, my francophone friend might interpret the menu for me, informing me that escargot are snails (at which point I order the bouillabaisse and the pouilly-fuissé instead). Beyond its linguistic meaning, I have already stated a sort of scholar's quick and dirty definition of interpretation above, "constructing and perpetuating meaning and in packaging meaning for consumption." Interpretation in the museum context has a fairly precise meaning. Ambrose and Paine define interpretation in the museum setting as follows:

> "Interpretation" usually means translating from one language to another. In the museum and heritage worlds, though, it has a special meaning: explaining an object and its significance. Almost everyone in the world, if shown a knife, will know roughly what it is meant to do: it is meant to cut. But if shown—for example—a Tibetan prayer wheel, most people will probably not have any idea what it is, and fewer still outside Tibet will know why or how it is used. To be fully understood and appreciated, an object needs to be interpreted or explained.[7]

Textile collections—rife with a controlled vocabulary of tools, terms, and techniques unfamiliar to the average person—need to be interpreted to be experienced and understood at their richest. Ask a museum visitor, whether in-house or online, for example, to define "turkey work"[8] and their answer might have something to do with poultry! "Bargello" (an Italian needlework technique) might as well be "escargot." Cue the menu again.

It is for this reason that WGBH Boston Media Library and Archives enlisted the help of scholars in the content areas of its back catalog of programs that it planned to release to the public in a digital, open access format online.

The Mellon Participatory Cataloging Project

WGBH, the PBS affiliate in Boston, received a grant from the Andrew W. Mellon Foundation to present to the public for the first time some of the back catalog of programs in WGBH's Media Library and Archives. The goal was to increase public awareness of the vast collections that digital repositories like WGBH hold by publishing their entire archival catalog in an online open access format on Open Vault, http://openvault.wgbh .org.[9] Getting all of these television programs digitized and up online was only the first step, however, as the catalog records for many of the programs were incomplete or simply did not exist. So, to improve the catalog records in order to make these old public television programs legible for contemporary viewing audiences, WGBH invited scholars to research one or more television series in WGBH's back catalog of programs and author metadata for each episode, along with linked media and a contextual essay. Below is a list of topics and programs that WGBH matched with scholars:

The life of Grete Bibring—student of psychoanalyst Sigmund Freud
The March on Roxbury, Mothers for Adequate Welfare, and the
    school Stay Outs taking place in Boston in the 1960s
Postwar television and *Joyce Chen Cooks*
The birth of MOOCs and IA Richards
Needlepoint with Erica Wilson
Radio personality Eric Jackson and his interviews with jazz masters
The legacy of Roger Fisher and his creation of the *Advocates*
The *Prospects of Mankind* featuring Eleanor Roosevelt and the
    anniversary of Kennedy's Report on the Status of Women
The Cold War and the *French Chef*
Poetry and technology
Tech nostalgia and moving image and sound heritage
Decade of the Brain—representations of the brain in public discourse
Violence in television—how violent media shapes research on human
    aggression
The African Liberation movement in the 1970s
Zoom—children's culture from 1965 to 1980

Being a historian of dress, textiles, and needlework, I was paired up with Erica Wilson's needlework program. Logically, a culinary historian was taken on to do Julia Child's seminal *French Chef* cooking program. And a historian of childhood worked on the metadata and essay for *Zoom*, a show that many readers of this book will no doubt remember from childhood. (Incidentally, the *Zoom* theme song was actually very helpful to me, because it includes the zip code for downtown Boston, "Boston, Mass, 02134!" I would think of it whenever I had to mail DVDs back to my project manager, saving me from having to look up the zip code there.)

As one of the scholars working on this participatory cataloging and curation project, I was tasked with watching every episode of *Erica* that could be digitized, tagging each episode with metadata of my choosing, and authoring an essay that would help scholars and viewers understand and use this collection of early public television craft shows. The following subsections provide background on the series and explore the logistics, benefits, and challenges of working remotely with a digital cataloging project, as well as briefly surveying the materials that I created for the project.

About the Series

Erica, also known as the *Erica Wilson Show*, was a television craft program produced by WGBH Boston. The show was hosted by Erica Wilson and ran from 1971 to 1972, and then 1975 to 1976, and was aired on PBS in the United States, the BBC in Britain, and also Australian television. *Erica* was one of the first, if not *the* first, craft shows on PBS. Wilson, who was born in England and grew up in Jamaica, was a graduate of the Royal School of Needlework in London. There, she learned numerous embroidery techniques, including crewelwork. Through her *Erica* television program, as well as her books and syndicated column, Wilson was instrumental in popularizing embroidery and needlepoint in the United States during the 1970s, a decade that saw a renewed interest in early crafts generally due to the Bicentennial.

The First Step: The Digitization Process

Below is a list of all of the episodes that WGBH managed to digitize. A third-party contractor did the digitization for this particular series out of house. Some episodes were not possible to digitize simply because they had already degraded to an extent that they were not useful for an open access project like this. So this was really a preservation project, an access project, a curatorial project, as well as an interpretive project. From the list of digitized episodes, one can see that we are missing episodes 102, 103, and 119 from Series One, and several from Series Two.

Series One

1971

Episode 101: Ticking Sampler
Episode 104: Bargello
Episode 105: Graphics from A to Z
Episode 106: Space Age Canvas
Episode 107: Turkey Work
Episode 108: Just Ties
Episode 109: Christmas Tree
Episode 110: Satin Stitch
Episode 111: Thinking Big
Episode 112: Designing Needlepoint
Episode 113: Chains
Episode 114: Thinking Bigger
Episode 115: Designs from China
Episode 116: Crewel Point
Episode 117: Shisha Work
Episode 118: Roumanian Stitch

1972

Episode 120: Sentiments in Stitches
Episode 121: Oriental Gold
Episode 122: Geometric Needlepoint
Episode 123: Cross Stitch
Episode 124: Needle Painting
Episode 125: Bell Pulls, Borders, and Bandings
Episode 126: Stitches in Needlepoint

Series Two

1975

Episode 201: Patchwork

1976

Episode 203: 3D Collage
Episode 209: New Points in Needlepoint
Episode 211: Native American Treasures
Episode 212: Fun, Fashion, and Costumes
Episode 213: Creatures Great and Small
Episode 215: Appliqué

Though most episodes of *Erica* deal with embroidery, I quickly discovered that Wilson made episodes on other textile arts as well, including quiltmaking. For example, episode 201 is on patchwork and 215 is on appliqué. Each episode features a showcase of museum pieces that provide inspiration for contemporary projects, which Wilson demonstrates. Various stitches are also demonstrated in each episode. Episodes from 1971 to 1972 are around 14 minutes in duration, while episodes from 1975 to 1976 last about 28 minutes.

Authoring and Submitting Interpretive Metadata

Now that we have established a bit about the show and the digitization process, let us move on to the scholars' roles in authoring and submitting metadata. (Yes, we have come full circle in this book, from preservation to interpretation, and we are still talking about metadata.) Each scholar was provided with a PDF guide on submitting metadata from the project manager at WGBH. The guide prescribed several fields, including the following:

Program title
Program summary (usually two or three paragraphs)
Topics (using Library of Congress subject headings when possible)
Duration
Color or black and white
Date aired
Date created
Copyright notice
Additional support provided by
People (including but not limited to producer, associate producer,
    director, performer, host, editor, writer, and music)

WGBH and Mellon were very flexible with regard to the metadata, allowing scholars the freedom to add new fields that we found important. I frequently added "episode number," "episode title," "selected textiles courtesy of" and "special thanks to." I also quickly noticed that many needlework-related terms are not easily written as a Library of Congress subject heading, so my project manager allowed me to create new subjects for terms such as "shisha" and "bargello." If you are an archivist, you may be cringing right now, thinking, "This is too inconsistent! What about interoperability of databases? What about Dublin Core?" But, as discussed in chapter 1, custom metadata vocabularies often allow for much richer searching of databases of textile collections. Though this project is a collection of episodes of a TV series, rather than a collection of material culture objects, because each episode is rife with terms from the world of textiles, the same rule applied. Scholars working on this interpretive project also enjoyed the fact that the metadata submission for this project was made very easy. Scholars were allowed to type everything up into a word-processing document, and then an intern at WGBH actually entered all of the metadata into the database. In fact, scholars on this project had no interaction with the back end of the site whatsoever.

Here is an example of the metadata entries that I created for episode 113, "Chains," an episode all about the chain stitch in embroidery (see figure 4.1). Note that the number of fields in this metadata scheme is quite small, and that the fields themselves correspond more or less to Dublin Core.

Program Title: Erica
Episode Number: 113
Episode Title: Chain

Figure 4.1.   Chain stitch embroidery and false quilting on a women's dress bodice, England or India, circa 1730–1760. Los Angeles County Museum of Art collection.

Program Summary: Chain stitch is an embroidery technique in which consecutive looped stitches form a chain pattern. Erica notes that chain stitch comes from the East and has been practiced in India for thousands of years. In this episode, Erica wears a dress made recently in India and decorated with chain stitch in silk. She shows many other traditional and contemporary Indian textiles—all of which were done in chain stitch, including two rugs made in Kashmir. Erica demonstrates how to do chain stitch with thick wool yarn using a crochet hook.

Topics: Needlework—Instruction; Embroidery; Chain Stitch; India—Decorative Arts; Clothing and Textiles—India

Duration: 00:14:27

Color or B&W: Color

Dates Aired:

Dates/Era Portrayed:

Date Created: 1971

Locations Portrayed:

Copyright Notice: Erica Wilson and Copyright WGBH Educational Foundation

Additional Support:

People (please note that some people vary from episode to episode—this is not just copied and pasted!): Host—Erica Wilson; Producer—Margaret MacLeod; Director—James Field; Set Designer—Frances Mahard

Selected Textiles Courtesy Of: Not stated

Some episodes, like "Chains," tended to be quite focused. Others, like episode 213, "Creatures Great and Small," covered a lot of territory, necessitating the production of a great many topics for the interpretive metadata:

Topics: Needlework—Instruction; Wildlife—Photography; Animals—Decorative Arts; Lions—Decorative Arts; Kittens—Decorative Arts; Chessie System; Chessie Kitten—Logos; Railroads—Logos—Needlework; Needlepoint; Crewelwork; Turkey Work; Animals—Habitat—Conservation; Noah's Ark; Potter, Beatrix; Animals—Children's Literature; Mice—Decorative Arts; Mrs. Tittlemouse; Ross, Betsy; Needlework—Colonial Revival; Peter Rabbit; Squirrel Nutkin; Stuffed Animals; Garden of Eden; Bible Stories—Decorative Arts; Appliqué; Birds—Decorative Arts; Decorative Arts—United States—19th Century; Whitework; Embroidery; Quilts; Organdy; Rabbits—Decorative Arts

The program summary for that episode is similarly lengthy.

Program Summary: In this episode, Erica goes on a "needlework safari," depicting various animals in stitchery. Erica shows how to translate wildlife photography via tracing paper onto needlepoint canvas, as well as how to select colored yarns that match the subtle variations in the colors of animals' fur and how to lengthen a split stitch to make it look more fur-like.

For the projects in this episode, she depicts lion and leopard cubs in needlepoint, the Chessie Kitten (the logo of the Chessie System, the holding company that owned the C&O and B&O railroads) [see figure 4.2] in crewelwork, as well as a pictorial embroidery depicting a rabbit, a fawn, and a prairie dog which states, "To love something is to give it room to grow." Erica notes about this piece that, like many people, she is very concerned about human population growth and the loss of animal habitat.

Erica also discusses needlework inspired by Bible stories and children's literature in this episode. She shows a rag book on Noah's Ark that she

Figure 4.2.   Chessie Kitten. Photo by Joe Haupt.

made for a young child, as well as needleworks that she did of Beatrix Potter characters including Mrs. Tittlemouse in crewelwork, Mrs. Tittlemouse
stitching the American flag in the guise of Betsy Ross, and free form Mrs.
Tittlemouse, Peter Rabbit, and Squirrel Nutkin dolls in heavy rug wool.

The first of the historical pieces shown in this episode is a needlework
depiction of the Garden of Eden done in New Jersey in 1874. The piece
features numerous appliquéd animals and birds. Erica uses this piece, as
well as children's drawings of animals, as inspiration for a naive bestiary
appliquéd wall hanging on linen. Erica also shows a whitework quilt from
1851 depicting a federal eagle. She takes this whitework quilt as inspiration
to do whitework embroidery of a rabbit on organdy.

Stitches demonstrated in this episode include tent stitch, lazy daisy stitch,
shadow work, split stitch (her preferred stitch for doing fur), and turkey
work, which Erica uses to make lions' manes and rabbits' tails bushy.

The final piece that each scholar contributed for the Mellon Participatory Cataloging Project was the scholarly, contextual essay. While it is
impossible to include that essay here, even in part, it may be found online
on the WGBH Open Vault website. A longer version of the essay was also
published in *Uncoverings*, the journal of the American Quilt Study Group.[10]

Interpretive Planning for the Web

How does one interpret in an online presentation, such as on a website?
One of the major challenges in interpreting two seasons of a television
series online was the dynamic versus static presentation. In terms of what
makes a good interpretive presentation online, I found that much of the
same best standards and practices for cultural institution's websites are
transferrable to sites created specifically for interpretive presentation of collections. In interpreting dynamic material online, the keys to the presentation of in the information seem to be *usability, quality, beauty and branding,
accessibility,* and *interaction.*

1. Usability: Is the site easy to navigate? Is the navigation where you
   would expect it to be? What about search functionality?
2. Quality, depth, and presentation: Do the online exhibitions reflect
   the breadth and depth of the institution, in terms of both subject
   matter and presentation of information? Does the quality of the
   online exhibitions reflect positively on the institution?
3. Beauty and branding: Does the aesthetic of the site (including color,
   fonts, and graphic elements) suggest that the museum/archive/

project offers a high-quality, mission-appropriate experience? Does it entice visitors to remain on the site?

4. Accessibility: Is the site available in multiple languages? Are there any special provisions made for the vision and hearing impaired?

5. Amount and type of user interaction permitted by the site: What is the extent to which the site embraces new innovation (e.g., links to social feeds, social tagging, etc.)?

As with interpretation in a traditional gallery space, however, factors to consider in interpretive planning include cost, conservation, custom, participation, and sustainability.[11]

Ultimately, though, interpretive planning should be purpose driven.[12] What is the aim of the interpretation? To impart information? To inspire creativity? To delight? Once the goal of the interpretation has been clearly articulated, interpretive planning, including the form(s) that the interpretation should take, naturally falls into place. In the case of *Erica*, WGBH wanted interpretation that was at once accessible to broad publics—researchers, students, teachers, and the general public—and imbued with a scholar's background knowledge and methodology. Given that these collections are housed at a public television station, rather than in a museum or university collection, it makes sense to seek the sort of authority normally ascribed to authors and scholars who can be said to be experts in their fields.

Writing and the implements that facilitate writing are some of the world's oldest technologies. Jay David Bolter has called the early twenty-first century the "Late Age of Print";[13] yet, with the rise of the Internet and social media, people are writing more than ever before. While this book has examined a myriad of technologies that impact work in dress and textile collections—from Babbage's Analytical Engine to contemporary social websites—one technology—writing—is the most overlooked but most vital of all.

A Need for Scholarly Interpretation

In scholarly discourse, interpretation (today more commonly called "cultural criticism") refers to the theory, methodology, or body of secondary source material privileged by the historian and used to make sense of the documentary or material past.[14] Italian historiographer Arnaldo Momigliano spoke of all evidence of the past as "data" and all secondary writing on that data as "interpretation."[15] In the examples in this chapter, individual episodes of *Erica* were the data, and the metadata and essay that I authored to contextualize them were the interpretation. At its core, interpretation really just is about providing context for some document or object that others may not be able to fully construct meaning from on their own. Of course, the ability to construct meaning varies from person to person and object to object. This is why, in my opinion, so-called overinterpretation is never a bad thing. When the object labels for a historic textile collection are presented in the manner of a traditional art museum or gallery (that is, with the bare minimum of information), visitors often struggle to construct meaning from what they see. People need interpretation.

In a seminal lecture on the interpretation of visual culture by art historian Sir E. H. Gombrich (1969), Gombrich beautifully defined scholarly interpretation through the example of interpreting a single footprint:

> To interpret a footprint means to match it in our mind with one of the creatures whose shapes and habits we know. The greater the repertoire of our knowledge and experience, the more likely we are to find the perfect fit. Sometimes, as we all know from detective stories, the fit may be literally perfect—a unique foot- or fingerprint may prove the presence of an individual at a certain spot. Sometimes, on the other hand, the fit will be more conjectural if, for instance, the tracks are less distinct or would fit several species. Occasionally, perhaps, the interpreter may be confronted by a track which sets his mind spinning. There is a story by Karel Capek of the single footprint on a wide virgin plain which is as mysterious as any miracle.[16] Where we cannot reconstruct, where we do not know what is possible, we cannot produce a convincing fit, we cannot interpret.[17]

A document or an object stumps even professional historians from time to time. This just a part of what makes historical research so exciting. And indeed, when I was first watched *Erica*, the resoundingly nostalgic character of the series struck me. Of course, the 1970s was the time of the Bicentennial and a national fascination with all things vaguely "colonial," but what surprised me was that just as often, if not more, Wilson turned her attention not to America's colonial needlework past but to the needlework of the trans-Atlantic Victorian period.

Perpetuating Meaning: Postmodernism's Victorian Afterlife

In this section, we will see myriad examples in which contemporary needlework culture perpetuates Victorian forms, styles, and techniques. Indeed, without postmodernism's so-called Victorian afterlife, peculiarly Victorian techniques like the macabre black cross-stitch might not be practiced

today. Perpetuation is very much like preservation in that to perpetuate
something—an idea, a craft, a family tradition, a mode of discourse—is to
keep it going into the future in perpetuity. We keep static objects going by
preserving them in museum and archival collections. But intangible things
such as those listed above cannot in most cases be physically put on a shelf.
Certainly, we can archive a video of them, and that is exactly what WGBH
Media Library and Archives did to preserve the *Erica* series—it digitized and
archived video of her making and teaching needlework. But to *perpetuate*
the series and its interpretation, one must do more than give historical context for content in the programs and define specialized needlework jargon;
one must also describe the practice and techniques of embroidery (as I will
attempt to do in the pages that follow) if visitors to the WGBH Open Vault
project are to be able to perpetuate the meanings they construct from the
Erica series themselves.

Good Old Victorian Clutter

Where did Erica Wilson's good old Victorian clutter come from? Lewis
Mumford opened his class study *The Brown Decades: A Study of the Arts in
America, 1865–1895*, first published in 1931 and reprinted in 1971 (the year
that the *Erica* series began its run on PBS), with these lines: "The com-
monest axiom of history is that every generation revolts against its fathers
and makes friends with its grandfathers. This reason alone might perhaps
account for the fact that the generation which struggled or flourished after
the Civil War now has a claim upon our interest."[18] Perhaps Wilson, who
was born in 1928, wanted to make friends with her great-grandparents. At
any rate, although it has been largely eclipsed by the colonial revival of the
Bicentennial, there was indeed a small Victorian revival in the 1970s, evidenced in a variety of media, such as jewelry, including Victorian-inspired
cameos, brooches, and cabochons.

Wilson's show, however, ostensibly catered to the modern woman
seeking to make modern needlework in the color palette of the 1970s—
acid yellows, pea greens, and the like—and using modern materials, such as
plastic needlepoint canvas and Lurex (a synthetic, metallic thread popular
in the period). Two modern, early and mid-twentieth-century develop-
ments, the Bauhaus and Charles and Ray Eames, must be mentioned as
transitional characters bridging the late nineteenth and the late twentieth
centuries. In *Women's Work: Textile Art from the Bauhaus*, Sigrid Weltge
notes that the weavers at the Bauhaus, despite working in an environment
that highly regarded industry and mass production as the future of mate-

rial culture, were seen as second-class citizens by their male counterparts in supposedly more technologically compatible disciplines. Weltge writes,

> The root of the conflict between handweaving and industry lay, at least in part, in their own uncertainty about their professional identity and also in the mixed messages they received from the masters, who saw weaving as women's work, and not part of a serious "male discipline." Industrial design, wedded to the "machine aesthetic," was just emerging in the mid-twenties and was, rightly or wrongly, often identified with the Bauhaus. Textile design, which shared equally in technological advances, consistently received, as it still does, little critical attention.[19]

That many of their fellow designers at the Bauhaus could not appreciate the way in which the Bauhaus weavers were breaking down the old binary divisions between textiles and technology, women's work and men's work, and craft and the machine, speaks to anxieties about the Industrial Revolution and the Cult of Domesticity that carried over from the nineteenth century into the twentieth, even into the Bauhaus itself.[20]

Charles and Ray Eames are also highly transitional figures in the history of design, and though they also worked to break down the barrier between textiles and technology in the public imagination, their artistic production can ultimately be read as post-Victorian. Though Charles and Ray Eames were trained in the early twentieth century and practiced throughout the middle of the twentieth century (1941–1978), they have, through their shared interests in digital technology, marginalized and non-Western populations, ornamentation, and vernacular culture, more in common with designers working in the period after 1975. Charles and Ray Eames had an extremely varied career, becoming distinguished in furniture design, architecture, toy design, graphic design, film, and new media. The Eameses were truly ahead of their time in their look (if there was such a thing), the wide scope of projects handled by their office, and their love of kitsch. The couple collected old mechanical toys, textiles, and other artifacts from various non-Western cultures, and numerous random doodads, littering most of the floor of their home with their treasures. Obviously, such behavior flew in the face of the rules of aesthetics of the high-style modernism of the mid-twentieth century. In the original House of Cards deck (1952), the pattern deck, each card was printed with a different pattern on its face, such as printed fabrics, Victorian découpage, or Asian papers. The second deck, the picture deck, consisted of cards with the faces printed with "good things," including sewing notions such as thimbles.[21] In fact, postmodern architect Robert Venturi claims that the Eameses "reintroduced good old Victorian clutter to interiors."[22]

Sentiments in Stitches

Postmodern culture (read: the culture of the 1970s and after in the West) is keenly aware of tradition and challenges tradition. The Italian medievalist and semiotician Umberto Eco characterized "the postmodern attitude as that of a man who loves a very cultivated woman and knows he cannot say to her, *I love you madly*, because he knows that she knows (and that she knows that he knows) that these words have already been written by Barbara Cartland."[23] The postmodern period is also witnessing the erosion of distinctions between high, folk, and popular visual expression.

The total breakdown of the barriers between high, folk, and popular culture is strongly in evidence on *Erica*. The projects in episode 120, "Sentiments in Stitches," for example, were jointly inspired by the character of Johnny Townmouse and William Shakespeare's *Love's Labours Lost*. This episode is all about stitching messages into one's embroidery work. The episode begins with Wilson showing several antique samplers, then moving on to showing some of her own work containing lettering, such as pictorial embroideries that she did of the illustrations and verses of Beatrix Potter's "The Story of Johnny Townmouse." Wilson also tells an anecdote of her girlhood in this episode, stating that she has always loved wildflowers and supposes that it dates from when she was seven years old and she and her school classmates were sent out into a field to pick wildflowers to bring back to the classroom for a flower-naming contest. This memory inspired Wilson to stitch embroidery with a wildflower motif. Around the central medallion containing the flowers, Wilson stitches the poem about flowers and springtime from Shakespeare's *Love's Labours Lost*:

> When daisies pied, and violets blue,
> And lady-smocks all silver-white,
> And cuckoo-buds of yellow hue
> Do paint the meadows with delight,
> The cuckoo then, on every tree,
> Mocks married men.[24]

Stitches demonstrated in this episode are the backstitch, which Wilson says is the best for doing lettering, and the split stitch, which is good for doing cursive writing and signatures in stitches. Wilson also provides instruction on how to transfer lettering on paper into embroidery. The first step, she tells the viewer, is to write out the lettering on graph paper. Next, the lettering is transferred to trace paper, which is pinned directly onto the fabric. One stitches directly through the paper, and, in the end, the paper is torn away, leaving only the embroidered lettering. In keeping with Eco's Barbara Cartland quotation, this episode concludes with Wilson showing two different designs for heart-shaped pillows incorporating the word "Love," a Victorian-inspired design created by her daughter and a very geometric piece designed by her husband. She demonstrates how to make her daughter's version, and concludes the episode by noting that while such a pillow would make a wonderful Valentine's Day present, "Love is acceptable at any time of the year."

Very many divergent styles coexist relatively peacefully within postmodern art and design; there is no longer domination by one or a few aesthetics. The Victorian aesthetic, however, plays a disproportionately large role in contemporary needlework culture. An example of the convergence of several of these elements of postmodern, or post-Victorian, visual culture is episode 122, "Geometric Needlepoint," which is jointly inspired by 1960s op art and Victorian embroidery, such as "Berlin" wool work (see figures 4.3 and 4.4) and black cross-stitch. In this episode, Wilson demonstrates techniques for designing geometric needlepoint designs with an op art or *trompe l'oeil* effect. For design inspiration, she suggests looking at op art wallpapers (which were still popular at the time), museum pieces (Wilson shows the viewing audience an antique sampler that she brought from her alma mater, the Royal School of Needlework), and even the Union Jack. For the project in this episode, Wilson takes her inspiration from a Victorian piece of cross-stitch, and shows the viewer how to create a black lace effect entirely in counted cross-stitch. The next episode, number 123, "Cross Stitch," was a follow-up very much about technical skills in stitchery. Stitches demonstrated in this episode are cross-stitch and herringbone stitch. Wilson also shows how to use cross-stitch for lettering, how to interlace herringbone with a contrasting color, and how to do cross-stitch over blocks of satin stitch. Historical pieces shown include a Victorian tablemat depicting chimney sweeps in silhouette using entirely black cross-stitch.

Wilson also frequently mixed English Jacobean, Carolean, or William and Mary inspirations with Victorian ones, as she did in episode 107, "Turkey Work." Turkey work is a form of knotted embroidery that was popular in England during the seventeenth century. It was meant to be imitative of the pile and designs of Turkish carpets. Wilson suggests using a thick wool thread and a very large needle. Turkey work is begun with a series of backstitches, leaving loops packed tightly together. The loops are then cut for a shaggy, tufted effect, or occasionally left intact, as with an embroidery of peonies that she did. Turkey work can be used today

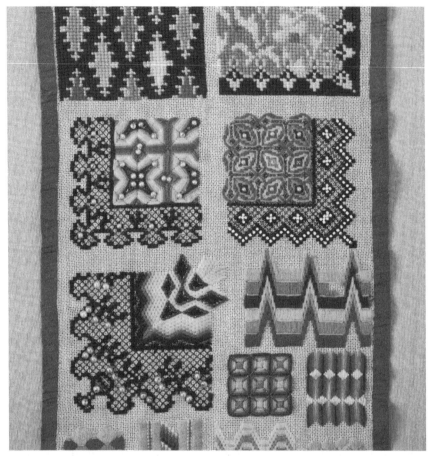

Figure 4.3.   Berlin wool work sampler, England, circa 1860. Los Angeles County Museum of Art collection.

to add texture and three-dimensionality to flora and fauna in embroidery, such as bumblebees or the centers of flowers. The project for this episode is an embroidered bumblebee with a turkey work body. Wilson cautions her audience to use straight stitches—not turkey work—for faces, and she shows a turkey work "Owl and the Pussycat" embroidery that she did, but with satin stitch eyes. She also shows a Victorian turkey work cockatoo from the Smithsonian.

We'll look at one final Victorianizing episode of *Erica*, episode 203, "3D Collage." This episode is all about creating works of embroidery in three dimensions. Wilson discusses two main ways to do such work—lightly padded and appliquéd forms and fully free-form pieces—and shows an example that she made of each, an embroidered owl with an appliquéd,

Figure 4.4.   Berlin wool work slippers, circa 1850–1900. Los Angeles County Museum of Art collection.

three-dimensional beak and fully free-form strawberries created out of fabric and batting. Wilson also shows several antique examples of three-dimensional needlework in this episode, including an eighteenth-century English stumpwork (raised embroidery) piece and a Victorian shadowbox containing a raised wool embroidery of wildflowers. Wilson demonstrates many stitches in this episode, including coral stitch, brushed wool stitch, and trellis stitch, as well as the technique for stumpwork and a technique for creating low-relief wildflowers out of pipe cleaners.

To Aestheticize Contemporary Reality

The computer, tablet, and smartphone are the new machines in the garden.[25] In the world of needlework, where the cool, sleek, and technological attributes of computers and the Internet are often at odds with the fuzzy and homespun self fashioning of the needlework population, Victorian design sensibilities can serve as a means of further humanizing the digital. Thus, as Kucich and Sadoff note, "aspects of late-century postmodernism could more appropriately be called 'post-Victorian.'"[26] Kucich and Sadoff argue that consumer culture uses the decorativeness and sentimentality of Victorian design to "aestheticize contemporary reality" as a means of humanizing the current digital age.

Consumer culture has shared in postmodern nostalgia for the nineteenth century, but—in contrast to Himmelfarb's politicized nostalgia—it uses the Victorian past to aestheticize contemporary reality. Victorian fashions and furnishings are enjoying a resurgence that has spawned magazines such as *Victoria* and *Victorian*. Home-decorating books [much in the style of East-lake's *Hints on Household Taste* from over a century earlier] and magazines teach twentieth-century homeowners how to load a mantle with curios and kitsch, people a wall with elaborately framed and sepia-toned family photos, and choose for the drawing room a patterned wallpaper or chintz.[27]

Erica Wilson's Victoriana pipe cleaner stumpwork can most certainly be interpreted in this way. Using the visual culture of the Victorian and Edwardian periods to "aestheticize contemporary reality" is also a crucial conceit in Judy Heim's *Needlecrafter's Computer Companion* (1995), an early guide to computers and the Internet for crafters.[28] *The Needlecrafter's Computer Companion* explores computing as applied to a wide variety of needle arts, including knitting, cross-stitch, needlepoint, and dressmaking.[29] Each chapter begins with a Victorian-looking illustration—the very Victorian nature of the illustrations in *Needlecrafter's Computer Companion* suggests that Heim understood a level of anxiety about technology among her readers. While Heim's text compares computers to the automobile in an attempt to make the computer seem more familiar, the illustration to her text depicts neither, but rather an even earlier technology—an early sewing machine. Taking the illustration into account, rather than reading, "Computers are not unlike cars," the text might read, "Computers are not unlike early treadle sewing machines with a woman in nineteenth-century garb seated serenely at them."

Throughout the book, Heim uses another visual device—the cherub. Perhaps even more Victorianizing than the nineteenth-century woman seated at the sewing machine are the cherub illustrations that can be found in each chapter of *The Needlecrafter's Computer Companion*. The cherubs are posed with neither computers nor quilts nor sewing machines, but rather with classical objects, such as the title page cherub's dramatic mask. Again, as with Luddites, Ruskin, and William Morris, the entrance of a new technology into the realm of textiles causes a disquiet that is allayed by what is seen as a return to the material and visual culture of a bygone era in which the technology had not yet been created. What the plethora of Victorianizing illustrations in Judy Heim's *Needlecrafter's Computer Companion* have in common are the depictions of Victorian motifs as a means of humanizing, minimizing, and anachronizing the computer. Kucich and

Sadoff write that "the technologies of postmodern media culture fetishize or are haunted by Victorian cultural documents."[30]

Related to the Victorian imagery in this computer guide for needle-crafters is historical costuming, especially the Victorian and Edwardian steampunks. Heim herself makes mention of online mailing lists for historical costumers, fantasy and science fiction costuming, "serious" Halloween and Mardi Gras costuming, and, finally, furry costuming.[31] Steampunk is a subgenre of science fiction or fantasy that has had a cult following since around 1990. Steampunk fiction is set in Victorian or Edwardian Britain (when steam power was still prevalent), but it also combines fantasy elements such as future technologies as Victorians might have imagined them. Babbage's protocomputer, the Analytical Engine, for instance, has figured prominently in works in the genre in which "postmodern rewritings of the Victorian fascination with information technologies or protocomputers— with 'difference engines'—revisit a period when the boundary between science and culture was unstable, when new technologies 'troubled the human/machine interface.'"[32] In the early twenty-first century, steampunk is not only a literary movement but also a live action role-play (LARP) movement. People craft Victorian clothing with future technological elements included for real-life conventions that they attend in character. Summer 2015 even saw a steampunk-fashion-oriented reality show on the Game Show Network, *Steampunk'd*.

Dressing up Victorian, Edwardian, or steampunk, and decorating one's home in those styles, is a common preoccupation in the virtual world *Second Life* among those who choose to role-play. Much of the branding of fabric and notions shops as well as other stores, such as antique shops, is geared to cultivating an image of virtual Victoriana. Griss's General Store brands itself as an "Authentic General Store with items for your RP [role-play], Victorian, or Antique home," according to their in-world profile. Not a true general store in the historical sense, the store sells finished crafts such as virtual quilts, clocks, furniture, and porcelain rather than traditional dry goods such as flour or fabric. According to Jennifer Green-Lewis, "Visual culture has currently identified the be-whiskered, top-hatted, and hoopskirted Victorians as appropriate objects for accumulating and expressing postmodern anxieties about authenticity."[33] In the virtual world, in which interaction is through first a computer terminal and then an avatarized self, such anxieties about technology and authenticity are no doubt heightened, perhaps explaining the popularity of Victorian visual culture in *Second Life*.

The relationship between textiles and technology has been fraught with anxiety since the early nineteenth century, when the historically infamous Luddites smashed the looms on industrializing woolen mills in northern England, and Babbage and Lovelace worked on a protocomputer that used the punch cards of those looms to weave the digital. "Thus Victorian technical forms continue to rewrite the present even as some theorists have tried to close their history by affirming, in extravagant terms, the radical newness of postmodern knowledge and computing technology."[34] The incursion of technology into the realm of textiles and vice versa represents an incursion of technology into the home and the family, and a perceived threat to the quality and beauty of the decorative arts. In the nineteenth century, by clinging to an imagined past filled with ideals of the pastoral and bucolic nature of the preindustrial countryside and the pure and subservient colonial woman at work at her spinning wheel, or, in the present day, to the sentimental Victorians and their arts and crafts movement, we alleviate our anxieties about the places where textiles and technology intersect.

Consuming Meaning: Shopping for History Online

Anxiety about the technological is one cultural marker of our own time. Another is, as Jean Baudrillard rightly noted, that it is not production, as Karl Marx believed, but rather consumption around which contemporary culture is oriented.[35] Much of this chapter, and indeed much of this book, has skirted around the role of consumption and consumer culture. Fashion and accessory goods included in Polyvore collections, craft programs like *Erica*, even museum exhibitions themselves are, first and foremost, created to be consumed by the public. Jerome de Groot noted that "the visual past is part of contemporary (global) consumption practice, one of many particular tropes deployed to encourage brand recognition and subsequent economic investment. History is co-opted here as part of the service industry, encouraging the consumer; it is not commodity itself but part of marketing and commodification."[36] If we are to believe Baudrillard's claim that consumption, not production, is the order of the day, then we can assume that if people truly connect with our interpretation—if they are able to construct meaning and want to perpetuate that meaning—they are much more likely nowadays to want to *buy* a product in the style of the topic of the exhibition rather than *make* one. Concert promoters know this well. People who have enjoyed consuming a meaning-making experience want to consume it again in the form of a souvenir (the word *souvenir*, of course, comes from the French for a memory or remembrance). That $10 program and $50 T-shirt? Totally worth it. Everyone who has ever worked in a museum gift shop—especially one strategically placed at the end of a major exhibition—knows this to be true. Moved by that Matisse exhibition? Then you probably want this *Bonheur de Vivre* print scarf.

I was doubtful that this need to consume that we feel after an experience in the brick-and-mortar world, such as a concert or museum exhibition, translated itself to online experiences. And I had given the matter no small amount of thought after all of my interpretive materials for the *Erica* series went live on the WGBH Open Vault site. After seeing *Yves Saint Laurent + Halston: Fashioning the 70s* (discussed in chapter 3) online, however (I could not make it to New York), I inexplicably found myself some days later wanting to buy a bottle of Halston perfume that I happened to see in the health and beauty aisle at my local mega-supermarket. This is likely not what curators Patricia Mears, Emma McClendon, and Fred Dennis intended, but the outcomes of museum visits—even online visits—are incredibly complex and very much bound up in human nature.[37]

This begs the question: If my interpretive materials for *Erica* are successful, how, then, are people consuming *Erica* post (online) visit? In her long career, Wilson published numerous needlework kits—many of which are available on eBay or may be found in antique shops or thrift stores. She also published some sixteen books, including *Crewel Embroidery* (1962), which sold over one million copies on its own.[38] Though Wilson passed away in 2011, her Erica Wilson flagship stores on Madison Avenue in New York City and on Nantucket are still open, selling reproductions of Wilson's needlework kits, along with such items as paintings of her work, tote bags, and jewelry.[39] There are certainly many ways for visitors to the WGBH Open Vault project to consume *Erica* in a material sense if they have made a connection with the series. Is this a good thing?

Shopping as Cultural Pursuit

In 1987, artist Barbara Kruger turned the iconic Enlightenment statement of self-affirmation by seventeenth-century French philosopher René Déscartes, "I think, therefore I am," into a seemingly dystopian mantra for the yuppie: "I shop, therefore I am." Is it so wrong to define oneself, at least in part, if not in sum, by that which one chooses to buy? Inherent in consumption is choice, and these consumer choices are predicated upon one's own personal values and aesthetic sensibilities. Indeed, shopping may now be understood as a cultural pursuit in its own right. In his essay

"Watteau, Art and Trade," Stephen Bayley noted, "Shopping has been described as one of the legitimate cultural pursuits of the 1980s, while at the same time, traditional museums are realizing the hidden value of their collections, treating them not merely as cabinets of curios, nor even as a scholarly resource, but ever more frequently as assets which can be reproduced, merchandised and marketed."[40] Bayley saw in the cultural sector of the 1980s a particular shift under way—a shift toward a middle-class consumerist ethic (and a shift that I would argue is strongly manifest in the 2010s). "This historical moment is one of very specific character, but does it mean—with shops becoming more sensitive to the market-place—that civilisation is under threat, that the values so carefully nurtured by a discriminating elite are menaced by barbarous populism, born of politically inspired consumerism?"[41] Hardly. In fact, consumerism has been hard at work in the cultural sector for centuries.

One of the most well-known paintings of the eighteenth-century rococo is not a painting in the traditional Western sense at all (that is, painted to be hung and admired as a work of art with no other purpose). Instead, Jean-Antoine Watteau's *The Signboard of Gersaint* was created to be—as its name suggests—a signboard. Watteau made the painting to serve as the signage for the Paris art gallery of Edmé-François Gersaint. So admired was the painted sign that Gersaint took it down and sold it a mere fifteen days after the work was installed as his gallery's signboard.[42]

There is perhaps no more trenchant symbol of shopping as a cultural pursuit—and of the blurring of the lines between art and commerce—however, than that of the Bon Marché. The Bon Marché, one of the great Parisian department stores—the quintessential symbol that the bourgeoisie had arrived—was completed in 1878. Pictured is a display window of the Bon Marché photographed around 1926–1927 by celebrated French photographer Eugène Atget (see figure 4.5). The rise of the department store in Paris in the nineteenth century was largely a result of the rising primacy of the bourgeois class as the determinants of culture. The urban, professional middle class was the new aristocracy, and they needed new institutions reflecting what had made their class great: beauty through simplicity and function, fueled by commerce and industry.

The department store was still a very new phenomenon in the 1870s. Its predecessor, a sort of dry goods store known as a *magasin de nouveautés*, had developed in the 1830s as the old guild system died out. These new stores used advertising and competitive pricing to draw customers, tactics that the guild system had not allowed to flourish.[43] By the 1870s, however, Paris had become a center of material consumption, and there was no shortage

Figure 4.5.   The Bon Marché, photographed by Eugène Atget, 1926 or 1927. George Eastman House collection.

of buyers or products. Instrumental in the rise of the department store as cultural form was the development of *prêt-à-porter* (also known as ready-to-wear or off-the-rack) clothing. Whereas the old *magasins de nouveautés* had sold dressmaking fabric, *prêt-à-porter* apparel called for a new type of store and a new type of shopping experience more focused on enticing the consumer to buy. Merchandise catalogs developed in the middle to late nineteenth century, playing an important role in marketing the goods of these new, large stores. The invention of chromolithography in the late nineteenth century made goods in catalogs look even more appealing.

Early in the nineteenth century, shops had been brought together and their streets covered to form a sort of pedestrian shopping plaza, such as the Passages des Panoramas. The Bon Marché became more of an icon, perhaps because it was one large store rather than a conglomerate of many, and, architecturally speaking, it was meant to be dramatic—not just a place to shop but also a place to see and be seen. The identity of the store was very much connected to the Boucicaut family, the owners of the Bon Marché, through the use of the family name on posters and other popular images. A visit to the store became a metaphorical visit to the Boucicauts themselves, linking the act of shopping with that of socializing with a high-profile family.

The design concept of the Bon Marché was based on function, beauty without artificiality, and the casting of the department store as a great stage on which the human drama of the mundane could unfold. The store's architects made use of another new technology, iron and glass construction, which, unlike the more popular Beaux Arts style, with its stone façades and classicizing ornament, was efficient to build and relatively inexpensive, and it seemed to embody the modern bourgeois spirit of progress. It was a new kind of architecture for a new kind of building with a new kind of clientele. No material other than iron would have been suitable for the Bon Marché. Iron itself was a product of the nineteenth century and prefabricated in factories owned by the bourgeoisie. This new construction method blurred the once firm distinction between the architectural form acceptable for a stylish boutique and that of a factory.

The current Bon Marché stands on the site of a former, smaller store of the same name. The original Bon Marché was one of the many stores built on the Rue de Sevres during the reign of Napoleon III. Owner Aristide Boucicaut decided that the store had to be rebuilt completely because he did more business than his small space with a complicated, confusing floor plan could accommodate. Louis-Auguste Boileau was chosen in 1867 to create a new, larger, simpler Bon Marché using iron and glass. The store was completed eleven years later (construction having been interrupted by the Franco-Prussian War) with the help of engineer Gustave Eiffel. The finished store was bordered by streets on all four sides and 10,000 square meters in area, the world's largest department store for many years.[44] When it finally opened in 1878, the new Bon Marché must have seemed absolutely huge, a modern, industrial temple to shopping. Émile Zola shared this view in his novel *Au Bonheur des Dames* (often translated as "The Ladies' Paradise" or "The Ladies' Delight"), a book largely set at the Bon Marché: "Everywhere he achieved space, air, light entering freely; the public circulated at ease under the bold lancing of long-span trusses. It was the Cathedral of modern commerce, solid and light, made for a congregation of clients."[45] The analogy of the feeling of being in the Bon Marché to that of being in a place of worship is indicative of the attitude of fin-de-siècle bourgeois Parisians. The act of consumption had already replaced the act of worship (and even the act of production) as the driving force of middle-class French society. The Bon Marché, however, was not only a temple of shopping; for decades it was *the* store, an institution that transcended its commercial purpose and became a cultural icon.

From Interpretation to Ownership

In the case of the Bon Marché, it was new technologies—including iron and glass construction, chromolithography, and *prêt-à-porter* apparel—that led to a transformation in the way in which people consumed fashion objects. In the museum world, we may well be at the edge of a precipice, on the verge of a change as significant as the shift from the dry goods stores—the *magasins de nouveautés*—to the department store. In the foreword to *Commerce and Culture*, Stephen Bayley wrote:

> Once, commerce and culture were all one. In the future it looks as though they will be one again. This startling assertion was stimulated by the curious observation that the gap between shops and museums is closing. Shops are becoming more "cultural," as anybody who has been to Ralph Lauren's Madison Avenue store can testify. Here you find merchandise for sale side-by-side with a permanent exhibition about values and style, set in an environment somewhat reminiscent of the Frick. Meanwhile, a few blocks away in the Metropolitan Museum, the first thing you hear when you cross the threshold is the whirr of cash-registers, evidence of a mighty commercial machine running at considerable speed. Shops and museums have a great deal in common. Urban, predominantly middle class, dedicated to exhibition, committed to consumption, either of images, ideas or goods. Once separated only by the availability of their contents (for sale in the stores, only for display in the museums), new attitudes and new technologies tend to erode this distinction between merchandise and collections.[46]

Technology—specifically, online shopping and social sites—may soon allow visitors to actually purchase museum collections.

In the future, it is very likely that those in the museum world will witness a significant breakdown of the distinction between goods and objects. "Knowledge is valuable and both shops and museums are realising it. Shops by adding quality of experience to the banal exchange of goods for money; museums by selling information and maybe, one day, even selling objects too."[47] And the future may be nearer than we think. Alexandra Palmer, senior curator of the *Textile and Costume* collection of Toronto's Royal Ontario Museum, has proposed an "adopt a dress" scheme for dress objects requiring conservation prior to exhibition.

> Another initiative would be to orchestrate an "adopt a dress" programme. Once the artefacts for exhibition and photography are identified, the project could be funded by virtually reselling the dress so the conservation of each design would be funded and recognised within the exhibition. In this manner, both moderate and more extensive conservation time and costs would be attached to each artefact slated for exhibition. The designs could be virtually "sold" to patrons who would underwrite the cost. Their names

would feature on the catalogue and object label as contributors to the longevity of the piece. The selection and cost of dresses would be wide: would you like to sponsor a Worth, O'Brien or Lanvin?[48]

Who wouldn't like to buy a share in a Lanvin? Pictured are a pair of Lanvin frocks illustrated in the *Baltimore and Ohio Employees Magazine* (1912) (see figure 4.6). Realistically, although there are certain to be

Figure 4.6.   Lanvin frock illustrated in the *Baltimore and Ohio Employees Magazine*, 1912. University of Maryland, College Park.

philanthropically motivated fashion enthusiasts out there, many individuals would rather take possession of the object that they have purchased. The democratic ideal of the online world might well be more oriented toward individual users than the civic organizations of the brick-and-mortar world.

High-end retail shopping websites like Net-a-Porter[49] and Zappos Couture[50] entice the consumer in a way that museums (whether it be an exhibition or the museum shop, in the brick-and-mortar world or online) often fail to do. How can the museum use technology to allow visitors to consume not only experiences but also objects? How can the museum website become more like a high-end retail website? How can the museum itself become more like a high-end retail store? These are all questions that face the contemporary historian, especially in fields such as historic dress studies and material culture that are already so dominated by the tactile and the thrill of ownership.

Through interpretation, the historian has the power to mitigate the understanding of history as an economic trope and reinvigorate the non-monetary values of historical objects. According to social and political historian Patrick Joyce, "'History is not commodity' and that the historians must stand firm 'against the market power of the mass, capitalist market.'"[51] Historians, however, also have a unique opportunity (and a responsibility) to recognize that consumerism and commercialization is—whether we like it or not—a strong narrative in contemporary Western society. Accepting and embracing this shift in museum practice will likely be a key skill for museum professionals going forward in the twenty-first century.

The Legend of Rip Van Recluse

Stephen Weil, one of the key figures in American museology in the twentieth century, warned against the danger of and the ease with which a museum professional can become stuck in their ways during the course of their career:

> Among the perennially favorite American stories is Washington Irving's tale of Rip Van Winkle, the amiable New York farmer who fell into a profound sleep as a loyal subject of George III, woke up some twenty years later, and was astonished to find that he had become a citizen of an entirely new country called the United States of America. What had happened while he slept, of course, was a revolution. If we could shift that frame just slightly and conjure up instead an old-fashioned curator in a New York museum—a tweedy Rip Van Recluse—who dozed off at his desk some fifty years ago and woke up today, would his astonishment at the museum in which he found himself be any less? I think not.[52]

The effect of digital technologies in the museum world has indeed been revolutionary, and surely curators of the past could scarcely have imagined the new opportunities for preservation, access, curation, and interpretation of historic dress and textile collections. The revolution does not end here, though. Rather, it is just about to pick up steam. The changes still to be wrought in museum work in the course of the twenty-first century must be immense. As curators, historians, preservationists, collections managers, or educators, it is our job not to become a tweed-clad Rip Van Recluse.

Notes

1. Keith Jenkins quoted in Jerome de Groot, *Consuming History: Historians and Heritage in Contemporary Popular Culture* (London: Routledge, 2009), 1.
2. The Rolling Stones, *Exhibitionism*, http://www.stonesexhibitionism.com/exhibition/.
3. de Groot, 1.
4. de Groot, 3.
5. de Groot, 3.
6. de Groot, 1.
7. Timothy Ambrose and Crispin Paine, *Museum Basics*, 3rd ed. (London: Routledge, 2012), 119.
8. Turkey work has nothing to do with poultry, and is instead an English form of knotted embroidery.
9. WGBH Open Vault, http://openvault.wgbh.org.
10. Amanda Grace Sikarskie, "Erica Wilson and the Quilt Revival," *Uncoverings*, 36 (2015).
11. Ambrose and Paine, 122.
12. Ambrose and Paine, 120.
13. Martin K. Foy, *Virtually Anglo-Saxon: Old Media, New Media and Early Medieval Studies in the Late Age of Print* (Gainesville: University of Florida Press, 2007), 2.
14. Charles S. Singleton, ed., *Interpretation: Theory and Practice* (Baltimore: Johns Hopkins University Press, 1969), v.
15. Arnaldo Momigliano, "Origins of the Roman Republic," in *Interpretation: Theory and Practice*, ed. Charles S. Singleton (Baltimore: Johns Hopkins University Press, 1969), 4–5.
16. The story by Capek that Gombrich refers to here is "Der Fußstapfen" (1918). The idea of a lone footprint in a hitherto untouched plain is derived from philosopher David Hume.
17. E. H. Gombrich, "The Evidence of Images," in *Interpretation: Theory and Practice*, ed. Charles S. Singleton (Baltimore: Johns Hopkins University Press, 1969), 36.
18. Lewis Mumford, *The Brown Decades: A Study of the Arts in America, 1865–1895*, 2nd ed. (New York: Dover, 1971), 1.

19. Sigrid Wortmann Weltge, *Women's Work: Textile Art from the Bauhaus* (San Francisco: Chronicle Books, 1993), 98.

20. For a larger discussion of the Industrial Revolution and the Victorian Cult of Domesticity, refer to chapter 1.

21. John Neuhart, Marilyn Neuhart, and Ray Eames, *Eames Design* (New York: Harry N. Abrams, 1989), 169.

22. Pat Kirkham, *Charles and Ray Eames: Designers of the Twentieth Century* (Cambridge, MA: MIT Press, 1995), 21.

23. Umberto Eco, *Postscript to "The Name of the Rose"* (New York: Harcourt, 1984), 530–31.

24. William Shakespeare, "Song of Spring," *Love's Labours Lost* (1598), http:// shakespeare.mit.edu/lll/full.html.

25. For a discussion of the term "machine in the garden," see Leo Marx, *The Machine in the Garden: Technology and the Pastoral Ideal in America* (New York: Oxford University Press, 1964).

26. John Kucich and Dianne F. Sadoff, eds., *Victorian Afterlife: Postmodern Culture Rewrites the Nineteenth Century* (Minneapolis: University of Minnesota Press, 2000), xii.

27. Kucich and Sadoff, xiii.

28. Judy Heim, *The Needlecrafter's Computer Companion* (San Francisco: No Starch Press, 1995).

29. A related work to *The Needlecrafter's Computer Companion* is Judy Heim and Gloria Hansen's *The Quilter's Computer Companion* (1998). In the late 1990s, Heim and Hansen offered quilters commonsense information about why they need a computer, how to use a computer and peripherals, the best software for specific quilting needs, the best software for use with an "old clunker" of a computer, using software to update the design of traditional old block styles, using software to aid sewing, embroidery, and appliqué, and using software for phototransfer onto fabric. The final chapter of *The Quilter's Computer Companion* diverges quite a bit from the rest of the book, telling quilters what they might do in cyberspace. Again, this provides a valuable introduction into how quilters were using the Internet at that time. The authors provide advice on finding fellow quilters one already knows in cyberspace, meeting quilters one has never met offline, finding quilt patterns, finding advice and feedback, downloading patterns, and even setting up a fabric or sewing notions shop online. Since this book is over ten years old, this information could feel very dated, and in some ways it does, but in many ways the information is still very useful because the authors focus on what one can do online rather than specific technologies or websites. One of the appendixes of this book is also quite valuable for the study of quilts and the digital: Christopher Holland's "The Quilter's Internet Yellow Pages." He breaks up the listings into categories such as websites, list-based discussion groups, clubs and guilds, swap groups, zines, sewing machine information, and so forth.

30. Kucich and Sadoff, xxiii.

31. Heim, 371–73.

32. Kucich and Sadoff, xxiii.

33. Kucich and Sadoff, xxiii.

34. Kucich and Sadoff, xxiii.

35. Jean Baudrillard, *The Mirror of Production*, trans. Mark Poster (New York: Telos Press, 1975).

36. de Groot, 10.

37. John Falk and Lynn Dierking established that visitors continue to construct new, intensely personalized (and impossible to predict) meanings from exhibits months after viewing them through postvisit interviews conducted after middle-class women attended the Smithsonian's National Museum of Natural History. See Falk and Dierking, *Learning from Museums: Visitor Experiences and the Making of Meaning* (Walnut Creek, CA: Alta Mira Press, 2000), 3–10.

38. Sikarskie, "Erica Wilson and the Quilt Revival."

39. Erica Wilson Nantucket Boutique, http://www.ericawilson.com.

40. Stephen Bayley, "Watteau, Art and Trade," in *Commerce and Culture: From Pre-Industrial Art to Post-Industrial Value*, ed. Stephen Bayley (Tunbridge Wells, Kent: Penshurst Press, 1989), 7.

41. Bayley, 7.

42. Marilyn Stokstad and Michael W. Cothren, *Art History*, 5th ed. (Boston: Pearson, 2014), 908.

43. Michael B. Miller, *The Bon Marché: Bourgeois Culture and the Department Store, 1869–1920* (Princeton, NJ: Princeton University Press, 1981), 21.

44. Frances S. Steiner, *French Iron Architecture* (Ann Arbor: UMI Research Press, 1984), 59.

45. Émile Zola, quoted in translation in Steiner, 60.

46. Bayley, "Foreword," in *Commerce and Culture: From Pre-Industrial Art to Post-Industrial Value*, ed. Stephen Bayley (Tunbridge Wells, Kent: Penshurst Press, 1989), 5.

47. Bayley, "Watteau, Art and Trade," 7.

48. Alexandra Palmer, "A Bomb in the Collection: Researching and Exhibiting Early 20th-Century Fashion," in *The Future of the 20th Century: Collecting, Interpreting and Conserving Modern Materials*, eds. Cordelia Rogerson and Paul Garside (London: Archetype, 2006), 47.

49. Net-a-Porter, http://www.net-a-porter.com/.

50. Zappos Couture, http://couture.zappos.com.

51. Patrick Joyce quoted in de Groot, 5.

52. Stephen Weil, *Making Museums Matter* (Washington, DC: Smithsonian Institution Press, 2002), 81.

Postscript   **5**
Meditations on Kate Middleton's Wedding Dress

IN THIS BOOK, I HAVE MADE NO GREAT EFFORT TO CONVINCE the reader of the importance of textiles and dress as historical documents that ought to be better preserved, accessed, curated, and interpreted for the public. I assume, reader, that if you have made it this far through an academic book on textile collections (and thank you very much for doing so), you feel, as I do, that these objects are tremendously valuable historically, culturally, and artistically, and they must be cherished. Of course, not everyone feels this way about dress and textile collections. In fact, the still too regularly male-dominated world of the digital humanities sometimes scoffs at these objects. Certainly, digital success stories such as the Quilt Index and other projects profiled in this book exist, but so, too, do the digital debacles that expose a persistent lack of gender equity. A famous example of this was the controversy over the denial of the inclusion of an article on Kate Middleton's wedding dress (see figure 5.1) in *Wikipedia*.

I learned of this dispute, somewhat fittingly (and not a little ironically), while perusing Slate.com for summer fashion advice. In "How Kate Middleton's Wedding Gown Demonstrates Wikipedia's Woman Problem," Torie Bosch reported, "The day of the royal wedding, a Wikipedia article about the dress was flagged for deletion. This prompted an energetic debate, as you can see on the dress's 'article for deletion' page."[1] Editors debating the merits of the topic on the article's Talk page called Middleton's wedding dress "frankly trivial," not notable enough to be on *Wikipedia*, and even deprecatingly joked, "Will there be an article on her shoes, too?"[2] An article on Middleton's bridal footwear never did appear on *Wikipedia*. However, one can read about them on her page at *wikiFeet*, "the collaborative celebrity

Figure 5.1.   Replica of Kate Middleton's wedding dress displayed in Belfast, Northern Ireland. Photo by William Murphy.

feet website."[3] (She takes a US 8.5, by the way.) What is most interesting about that Wikipedian's comment about shoes, though, is that both male and female users are guilty of gender bias online.

Wikipedia, authored and edited entirely by a volunteer community online, can only be as encyclopedic as the interests and values of its contributors. So how does *Wikipedia* evaluate article topics for inclusion or deletion? *Wikipedia*'s own guidelines state that of prime import in whether an article on a topic may be included is the topic's *notability*. Recall that the second *Wikipedia* user quoted in the Bosch piece stated, "This is frankly trivial, and surely isn't notable enough to be on wikipedia." But one user's opinion was never intended to be the litmus test of notability. Rather, *Wikipedia* defines a notable topic as one that "has received significant coverage in reliable sources that are independent of the subject."[4] Surely the worldwide media hullabaloo surrounding the wedding of Prince William and Kate Middleton in 2011, including extensive coverage of both her dress and engagement ring (a twelve-carat blue sapphire that once belonged to Princess Diana), qualifies the dress as "notable."

As we have seen, however, determining notability is not so simple in practice, as the cultural biases of those making the determination must be taken into account. According to Bosch, "The same editors who deem those Linux articles [*Wikipedia* has over one hundred unique articles on Linux distributions] important might dismiss articles on makeup, say, as 'some fluffy girl topic'—despite significant cultural impact."[5] Digital humanities scholar Adrianne Wadewitz argues that this bias against so-called women's interest topics is part of a larger historical trend going back at least to the eighteenth century: "WikiProjects, which organize Wikipedia's content around topics to mobilize its editors, show the level of interest in a topic. The most organized and successful WikiProject is Military History while projects like Textile Arts languish. In many ways, Wikipedia suffers from the same exclusionary problems of the Encyclopédie of old."[6] Denis Diderot's enlightenment-era *Encyclopédie*, incidentally, was indeed much like today's *Wikipedia* in that while it did devote some entries to dress and textile topics (including velvet, brocaded fabrics, and bonnet making), the bulk of the work was on topics in natural and ecclesiastical history, philosophy, mathematics, physics, and literature.[7] This gender bias is not just a problem and a symptom of modernity, either, for while the *Encyclopédie* may have given short shrift to the textile arts, so did the oldest surviving encyclopedia: Pliny the Elder's *Naturalis Historia*, which dates to the first century CE and features a markedly similar breakdown of topics.[8] Let us indulge all of the naysayers both past and present for a moment and defend the notability of the dress and textile topics in general.

Why are wedding dresses, especially those worn by social elites, so very notable? In their introduction to *Wedding Dress across Cultures*, Helen Bradley Foster and Donald Clay Johnson note that in the history and ethnography of dress, the importance of the wedding dress is paramount: "Perhaps the most visible and telling of dress modes are wedding garments, the choice of which makes a statement by showing comparative prestige, wealth or perceived status."[9] The wedding dress is more than just a marker of the social, economic, or political status of the family of the wearer, however. According to Foster and Johnson, "In a larger sense, wedding dress forms a complex set of interlocking relationships that tie a society together as it unites a couple in marriage."[10] Essentially, wedding dresses can be read as a sort of cultural glue that binds society together.

Another test of notability is whether articles on comparable topics exist. A search of *Wikipedia* for entries on royal wedding dresses yields several results, including "Wedding Dress of Queen Victoria,"[11] "Wedding Dress of Princess Beatrice" (Queen Victoria's youngest daughter),[12] "Wedding Dress of Princess Elizabeth" (now Queen Elizabeth II),[13] "Wedding Dress of Princess Alexandra of Denmark,"[14] and even "Wedding Dress of Princess Mary of Teck."[15] Certainly there is a precedent for articles on royal wedding dresses on *Wikipedia*.

Many of the dresses listed above are notable for not only who wore them but also who made them. Sarah Burton designed the dress worn by

Middleton, now the Duchess of Cambridge, for Alexander McQueen, one of Britain's most famous luxury fashion houses. The dress also featured highly intricate embroidery executed by workers from the Royal School of Needlework (the same school that Erica Wilson, the subject of chapter 4, attended). The Victorian-inspired design, including a corseted bodice, echoed back to another famous royal wedding dress—that of Queen Victoria. When Victoria wed Prince Albert in 1840, she wore a dress made from white Spitalfields silk, cut with a then-contemporary silhouette, and a sapphire brooch given to her by Albert.[16] This continuity with the royal past is yet another marker of the dress's importance or notability.

One final marker of the significance of not just Middleton's dress or royal wedding dresses in general but nearly all traditional wedding dresses is their symbolism, with the color white standing for supposedly feminine virtues that society wished to cultivate in young women and secure through marriage. In England, the white wedding dress was firmly ensconced as tradition by the late eighteenth century.[17] "In Europe and North America, white, symbolizing 'purity,' remains the preferred color, a reflection of the pervasive power of English Victorian society to impose its value system throughout many parts of the world."[18] Effectively, Middleton's dress is a document of tremendous historical significance—in terms of its own design and artistry, its probable impact on fashion for years to come, but also because it is simultaneously a powerful symbol of both contemporary Britain and Britain's colonial and patriarchal past.

Ultimately, notability won the day in the case of Kate Middleton's wedding dress. Today, the *Wikipedia* article "Wedding Dress of Kate Middleton" presents information about pre-wedding speculation about the dress, as well as the dress's design, cultural reception, and influence.[19] But this episode serves as a stern reminder that while pursuits in which women play a major role dominate the contemporary Web, including (but certainly not limited to) social media and online shopping, "serious" digital projects from the digital humanities on down to *Wikipedia* are marred by a gender bias that serves to reduce access to content in dress and textile studies. Textiles and technology were intimate bedfellows at the genesis of digital computing. Projects such as those profiled in this book play a crucial role in reminding us that the binary logic of zeros and ones is really just the logic of warp and weft.

Notes

1. Torie Bosch, "How Kate Middleton's Wedding Gown Demonstrates Wikipedia's Woman Problem," Slate.com (July 13, 2012), http://www.slate.com/

blogs/future_tense/2012/07/13/kate_middleton_s_wedding_gown_and_wiki pedia_s_gender_gap_.html.

2. The article's Talk page, referenced by Bosch, may be accessed at https://en.wikipedia.org/wiki/Talk:Wedding_dress_of_Kate_Middleton.

3. "Kate Middleton's Feet," *wikiFeet: The Collaborative Celebrity Feet Website*, http://www.wikifeet.com/Kate_Middleton.

4. "Wikipedia: Notability," *Wikipedia*, https://en.wikipedia.org/wiki/Wikipedia:Notability.

5. Bosch.

6. Adrianne Wadewitz, "Wikipedia Is Pushing the Boundaries of Scholarly Practice But the Gender Gap Must Be Addressed," *HASTAC: Humanities, Arts, Science and Technology Alliance and Collaboratory* (April 9, 2013), http://www.hastac.org/blogs/wadewitz/2013/04/09/wikipedia-pushing-boundaries-scholarly-practice-gender-gap-must-be.

7. See Benjamin Heller and Marketa Kubacakova's translation and diagram of Diderot and d'Alembert's *Map of the System of Human Knowledge*, in *The Encyclopedia of Diderot and d'Alembert Collaborative Translation Project*, http://quod.lib.umich.edu/d/did/tree.html.

8. Pliny the Elder, *Pliny's Natural History*, trans. H. Rackham, W. H. S. Jones, and D. E. Eichholz, http://www.masseiana.org/pliny.htm#BOOK%20XXXV.

9. Helen Bradley Foster and Donald Clay Johnson, eds., *Wedding Dress across Cultures* (Oxford: Berg, 2003), 1.

10. Foster and Johnson, 1.

11. "Wedding Dress of Queen Victoria," *Wikipedia*, https://en.wikipedia.org/wiki/Wedding_dress_of_Queen_Victoria.

12. "Wedding Dress of Princess Beatrice," *Wikipedia*, https://en.wikipedia.org/wiki/Wedding_dress_of_Princess_Beatrice.

13. "Wedding Dress of Princess Elizabeth," *Wikipedia*, https://en.wikipedia.org/wiki/Wedding_dress_of_Princess_Elizabeth.

14. "Wedding Dress of Princess Alexandra of Denmark," *Wikipedia*, https://en.wikipedia.org/wiki/Wedding_dress_of_Princess_Alexandra_of_Denmark.

15. "Wedding Dress of Princess Mary of Teck," *Wikipedia*, https://en.wikipedia.org/wiki/Wedding_dress_of_Princess_Mary_of_Teck.

16. Shelley Tobin, Sarah Pepper, and Margaret Willes, *Marriage à la Mode: Three Centuries of Wedding Dresses* (London: The National Trust, 2003), 32.

17. Tobin, Pepper, and Willes, 20.

18. Foster and Johnson, 2.

19. "Wedding Dress of Kate Middleton," *Wikipedia*, https://en.wikipedia.org/wiki/Wedding_dress_of_Kate_Middleton.

Bibliography

Alcott, Louisa May. *Little Women*. New York: Dutton, 1948.

———. "Patty's Patchwork." In *Aunt Jo's Scrap Bag*, 194. Boston: Roberts Brothers, 1889.

AlexD. "Alex Dyer." Polyvore. http://alexd.polyvore.com.

———. "Donyale Luna." Polyvore. http://www.polyvore.com/donyale_luna/set?id=149298530.

Ambrose, Timothy, and Crispin Paine. *Museum Basics*. 3rd ed. London: Routledge, 2012.

Arvanitis, Konstantinos. "Museums Outside Walls: Mobile Phones and the Museum in the Everyday." In *Museums in a Digital Age*, edited by Ross Parry, 170–76. London: Routledge, 2010.

Atton, Chris. *An Alternative Internet*. Edinburgh: Edinburgh University Press, 2004.

Babbage, Charles. *On the Economy of Machinery and Manufactures*. New York: A. M. Kelley, 1963.

Babbitts, Judith. "Stereographs and the Construction of a Visual Culture in the United States." In *Memory Bytes: History, Technology and Digital Culture*, edited by Lauren Rabinovitz and Abraham Geil, 126–49. Durham, NC: Duke University Press, 2004.

Bachmann, Ingrid. "Material and the Promise of the Immaterial." In *Material Matters: The Art and Culture of Contemporary Textiles*, edited by Ingrid Bachmann and Ruth Scheuing. Toronto: YYZ Books, 1998.

Bachmann, Ingrid, and Ruth Scheuing, eds. *Material Matters: The Art and Culture of Contemporary Textiles*. Toronto: YYZ Books, 1998.

Barthes, Roland. *Camera Lucida*. New York: Hill and Wang, 1981.

Baudrillard, Jean. *The Mirror of Production*. Translated by Mark Poster. New York: Telos Press, 1975.

Bayley, Stephen. "Foreword." In *Commerce and Culture: From Pre-Industrial Art to Post-Industrial Value*, edited by Stephen Bayley, 5–6. Tunbridge Wells, Kent: Penshurst Press, 1989.

———. "Watteau, Art and Trade." In *Commerce and Culture: From Pre-Industrial Art to Post-Industrial Value*, edited by Stephen Bayley, 7–12. Tunbridge Wells, Kent: Penshurst Press, 1989.

Benjamin, Walter. "The Work of Art in the Age of Mechanical Reproduction." In *Commerce and Culture: From Pre-Industrial Art to Post-Industrial Value*, edited by Stephen Bayley, 34–38. Tunbridge Wells, Kent: Penshurst Press, 1989.

Berners-Lee, Tim. "The Next Web of Open Linked Data." TED Talks (February 2009). http://www.youtube.com/watch?v=OM6XIICm_qo.

———. "The Year Open Data Went Worldwide." TED Talks (February 2010). http://www.youtube.com/watch?v=3YcZ3Zqk0a8.

Bernstein, Shelley, et al. "Brooklyn Museum Collection, Posse, and Tag! You're It!" Paper presented at the annual conference on Museums and the Web, Indianapolis, Indiana, April 15–18, 2009.

Bohemians. "Style Inspiration: Anita Pallenberg." Polyvore. http://www.poly vore.com/style_inspiration_anita_pallenberg/set?id=73731085.

Bosch, Torie. "How Kate Middleton's Wedding Gown Demonstrates Wikipedia's Woman Problem." Slate.com (July 13, 2012). http://www.slate .com/blogs/future_tense/2012/07/13/kate_middleton_s_wedding_gown _and_wikipedia_s_gender_gap_.html.

Brackman, Barbara. *Encyclopedia of Appliqué*. Lafayette, CA: C&T Publishing, 2009.

———. *Encyclopedia of Pieced Quilt Patterns*. Paducah, KY: American Quilter's Society, 1993.

———. *Patterns of Progress: Quilts in the Machine Age*. Los Angeles: Autry Museum of Western Heritage, 1997.

Brecht, Bertolt. "Radio as a Means of Communication: A Talk on the Function of Radio." http://www.nyklewicz.com/brecht.html.

Brooks, Mary M., and Dinah Eastop, eds. *Changing Views of Textile Conservation*. Los Angeles: Getty Conservation Institute, 2011.

Bush, Vannevar. "As We May Think." *Atlantic Monthly* 176 (1945): 101–8.

Cameron, Fiona, and Sarah Kenderdine, eds. *Theorizing Digital Cultural Heritage*. Cambridge, MA: MIT Press, 2007.

Christian, Talula. *Talula Christian*. Tumblr. http://talulachristian.tumblr.com/.

Colby, Averill. *Patchwork*. London: Batsford, 1958.

Cole, Drusilla. *Textiles Now*. London: Lawrence King, 2008.

Corn, Joseph. "Object Lessons/Object Myths: What Historians of Technology Can Learn from Things." In *Learning from Things*, edited by W. David Kingery, 35–54. Washington, DC: Smithsonian Institution Press, 1996.

Cornwell, Regina. "From the Analytical Engine to Lady Ada's Art." In *Iterations: The New Image*, edited by Timothy Druckrey, 41–61. Cambridge, MA: MIT Press, 1993.

Cumming, Elizabeth. "Pure Magic: The Power of Tradition in Scottish Arts and Crafts." In *NeoCraft: Modernity and the Crafts*, edited by Sandra Alfoldy. Halifax: Press of the Nova Scotia College of Art and Design, 2007.

Cunningham, Michael. *Cirque du Fromage*. http://www.cirquedufromage.com/.

Dana, John Cotton. *The New Museum*. Washington, DC: American Association of Museums, 1999.

de Groot, Jerome. *Consuming History: Historians and Heritage in Contemporary Popular Culture*. London: Routledge, 2009.

Druckrey, Timothy, ed. *Iterations: The New Image*. Cambridge, MA: MIT Press, 1993.

Eames, Charles, and Ray Eames. *A Computer Perspective*. Cambridge, MA: Harvard University Press, 1973.

Eastlake, Charles. *Hints on Household Taste*. Reprint. New York: Dover, 1986.

Eco, Umberto. *Postscript to "The Name of the Rose."* New York: Harcourt, 1984.

Eiler, Lyntha Scott, Terry Eiler, and Carl Fleischhauer. *Blue Ridge Harvest: A Region's Folklife in Photographs*. Washington, DC: Library of Congress, 1981.

Elsley, Judy. "Making Critical Connections in Quilt Scholarship." *Uncoverings* 16 (1995): 229–43.

Escobar, Arturo. "Gender, Place and Networks: A Political Ecology of Cyberculture." In *Women @ Internet: Creating New Cultures in Cyberspace,* edited by Wendy Harcourt. London: Zed Books, 1999.

Essinger, James. *Jacquard's Web: How a Hand-loom Led to the Birth of the Information Age*. Oxford: Oxford University Press, 2004.

Falk, John H., and Lynn D. Dierking. *Learning from Museums: Visitor Experiences and the Making of Meaning*. Walnut Creek, CA: Alta Mira Press, 2000.

Fashion Illustration & Textiles. Tumblr. http://fashionillustration-textiles.tumblr.com/.

Fessenden, Marissa. "Computers Are Learning about Art Faster than Art Historians." *Smithsonian Magazine* (May 2015). http://www.smithsonianmag.com/smart-news/computers-are-getting-better-identifying-artists-art-historians-are-180955241/#aZ6yd84bC3eSt0id.99.

Fisher, Richard, and Dorothy Wolfthal. *Textile Print Design*. Fairchild Books and Visuals, 1987.

Fleming, Olivia. "Why the World's Most Talked-About New Art Dealer Is Instagram." *Vogue* (May 13, 2014). http://www.vogue.com/872448/buying-and-selling-art-on-instagram/.

Foster, Helen Bradley, and Donald Clay Johnson, eds. *Wedding Dress across Cultures*. Oxford: Berg, 2003.

Foxboro. "Swinging London." Polyvore. http://www.polyvore.com/swinging_london/set?id=24909796&lid=648523.

———. "Twiggy." Polyvore. http://www.polyvore.com/twiggy/set?id=24619170&lid=648523.

Foy, Martin K. *Virtually Anglo-Saxon: Old Media, New Media and Early Medieval Studies in the Late Age of Print*. Gainesville: University of Florida Press, 2007.

Frankel, Nicholas. "The Ecstasy of Decoration: The Grammar of Ornament as Embodied Experience." *Nineteenth Century Art Worldwide* 2, no. 1 (2003): 1–32.

Frankle, Elissa. "More Crowdsourced Scholarship: Citizen History." *Center for the Future of Museums Blog* (July 28, 2011). http://futureofmuseums.blogspot.com/2011/07/more-crowdsourced-scholarship-citizen.html.

Friedman, Ted. *Electric Dreams*. New York: New York University Press, 2005.

Fry, W. Logan. "Fiber in Cyberspace." *FiberArts* 27 (January/February 2001): 40–41.

Gansallo, Matthew. "Curating New Media." In *Museums in a Digital Age,* edited by Ross Parry, 344–50. London: Routledge, 2010.

Gaskell, Elizabeth. *North and South*. London: Oxford University Press, 1973.

Geijer, Agnes. "Preservation of Textile Objects." In *Changing Views of Textile Conservation,* edited by Mary M. Brooks and Dinah D. Eastop, 185–89. Los Angeles: Getty Conservation Institute, 2011.

Glaspell, Susan. "A Jury of Her Peers." Annenberg Lerner Literature Interactives. http://www.learner.org/interactives/literature/story/fulltext.html.

Glassie, Henry. "Meaningful Things and Appropriate Myths: The Artifact's Place in American Studies." *Prospects* 3 (1977): 1–49.

Gombrich, E. H. "The Evidence of Images." In *Interpretation: Theory and Practice,* edited by Charles S. Singleton. Baltimore: Johns Hopkins University Press, 1969.

Graham, Beryl. "Redefining Digital Art." In *Theorizing Digital Cultural Heritage: A Critical Discourse,* edited by Fiona Cameron and Sarah Kenderdine, 93–112. Cambridge, MA: MIT Press, 2007.

Gunn, Virginia. "From Myth to Maturity: The Evolution of Quilt Scholarship." *Uncoverings* 13 (1992): 192–205.

Harris, Mary. *Common Threads: Women, Mathematics and Work*. Stoke on Trent, UK: Trentham Books, 1997.

Harrod, Tanya. "Otherwise Unobtainable: The Applied Arts and the Politics and Poetics of Digital Technology." In *NeoCraft: Modernity and the Crafts,* edited by Sandra Alfoldy. Halifax: Press of the Nova Scotia College of Art and Design, 2007.

Hatch, Kathryn L. *Textile Science*. Minneapolis-Saint Paul: West Publishing, 1993.

Heidegger, Martin. *The Question Concerning Technology and Other Essays*. New York: Garland, 1977.

Heim, Judy. *The Needlecrafter's Computer Companion*. San Francisco: No Starch Press, 1995.

Heim, Judy, and Gloria Hansen. *The Quilter's Computer Companion*. San Francisco: No Starch Press, 1998.

Hicks, Kyra. *Black Threads: An African American Quilting Sourcebook*. Jefferson, NC: McFarland, 2003.

Hockey, Susan. "The History of Humanities Computing." In *A Companion to Digital Humanities,* edited by Susan Schreibman et al., 3–19. Oxford: Blackwell, 2004.

Horton, Laurel, ed. *Quiltmaking in America: Beyond the Myths*. Nashville, TN: Rutledge Hill, 1994.

Ivey, Bill. *Arts, Inc*. Berkeley and Los Angeles: University of California Press, 2008.

Jackson, Roland. "The Virtual Visit: Towards a New Concept for the Electronic Science Centre." In *Museums in a Digital Age,* edited by Ross Parry, 153–58. London: Routledge, 2010.

Jenkins, Henry. *Convergence Culture*. New York: New York University Press, 2006.

Jolliffe, Kira, and Bay Garnett. *The Cheap Date Guide to Style*. New York: Universe Publishing, 2008.

Jones-Garmill, Katherine, ed. *The Wired Museum: Emerging Technology and Changing Paradigms*. Washington, DC: American Association of Museums, 1997.

Jones, Stephen. *Against Technology: From the Luddites to Neo-Luddism*. London: Routledge, 2013.

Jönsson, Love. "Rethinking Dichotomies: Crafts and the Digital." In *NeoCraft: Modernity and the Crafts*, edited by Sandra Alfoldy. Halifax: Press of the Nova Scotia College of Art and Design, 2007.

July, Miranda. Learning to Love You More. http://www.learningtoloveyoumore.com/.

Kajitani, Nobuko. "Care of Fabrics in the Museum." In *Changing Views of Textile Conservation*, edited by Mary M. Brooks and Dinah D. Eastop, 161–80. Los Angeles: Getty Conservation Institute, 2011.

Keene, Suzanne. *Digital Collections: Museums and the Information Age*. Oxford: Butterworth-Heinemann, 1998.

Kingery, W. David, ed. *Learning from Things: Method and Theory of Material Culture Studies*. Washington, DC: Smithsonian Institution Press, 1996.

Kirkham, Pat. *Charles and Ray Eames: Designers of the Twentieth Century*. Cambridge, MA: MIT Press, 1995.

Kucich, John, and Dianne F. Sadoff, eds. *Victorian Afterlife: Postmodern Culture Rewrites the Nineteenth Century*. Minneapolis: University of Minnesota Press, 2000.

Lessig, Lawrence. *Code 2.0*. New York: Basic Books, 2006.

———. "Laws That Choke Creativity." TED Talks (March 2007). https://www.ted.com/talks/larry_lessig_says_the_law_is_strangling_creativity.

Lévy, Pierre. *Cyberculture*. Minneapolis: University of Minnesota Press, 2001.

Lilysue. "Donyale Luna." Polyvore. http://www.polyvore.com/donyale_luna/set?id=118430976.

MacArthur, Matthew. "Get Real! The Role of Objects in the Digital Age." In *Letting Go? Sharing Historical Authority in a User-Generated World*, edited by Bill Adair, Benjamin Filene, and Laura Koloski, 56–67. Philadelphia: Pew Center for Arts and Heritage, 2011.

MacDowell, Marsha, et al. "Quilted Together: Material Culture Pedagogy and the Quilt Index, a Digital Repository of Thematic Collections." *Winterthur Portfolio* 47, no. 2/3 (2011): 8–40.

Mao, Dong, Daniel N. Rockmore, Yang Wang, and Qiang Wu. "EMD Analysis for Visual Stylometry." *IEEE Transactions on Pattern Analysis and Machine Intelligence*. http://www.mth.msu.edu/~ywang/Preprints/EMD_Bruegel-IEEE.pdf.

Marden, Albert. *Outer Circles: An Introduction to Hyperbolic 3-Manifolds*. Cambridge: Cambridge University Press, 2007.

Martinez, Katharine, and Kenneth L. Ames, eds. *The Material Culture of Gender, The Gender of Material Culture.* Winterthur, DE: Henry Francis du Pont Winterthur Museum; Hanover: Distributed by University Press of New England, 1997.

Marty, Paul F., and Katherine Burton Jones, eds. *Museum Informatics: People, Information and Technology in Museums.* London: Routledge, 2008.

Marvin, Carolyn. *When Old Technologies Were New: Thinking about Electronic Communication in the Nineteenth Century.* New York: Oxford University Press, 1988.

Marx, Leo. *The Machine in the Garden: Technology and the Pastoral Ideal in America.* New York: Oxford University Press, 1964.

Mault, Coco. "Audrey Hepburn on the Moon." Flickr Commons, https://www.flickr.com/photos/contusion/7485321088/in/photolist-cpseb9.

McLean, Kathleen. "Whose Questions, Whose Conversations?" In *Letting Go? Sharing Historical Authority in a User-Generated World,* edited by Bill Adair, Benjamin Filene, and Laura Koloski, 74–76. Philadelphia: Pew Center for Arts and Heritage, 2011.

Melissa. *Incense and Peppermints.* Tumblr. http://thewonderfulworldofthe60s.tumblr.com/.

Menabrea, L. F. "Sketch of The Analytical Engine Invented by Charles Babbage, Esq." Translated by Ada, Countess of Lovelace. In *Scientific Memoirs* 3 (1843): 666–731.

Miller, Michael B. *The Bon Marché: Bourgeois Culture and the Department Store, 1869–1920.* Princeton, NJ: Princeton University Press, 1981.

Momigliano, Arnaldo. "Origins of the Roman Republic." In *Interpretation: Theory and Practice,* edited by Charles S. Singleton. Baltimore: Johns Hopkins University Press, 1969.

Moore, Doris Langley. *Ada, Countess of Lovelace: Byron's Legitimate Daughter.* New York: Harper & Row, 1977.

Mumford, Lewis. *The Brown Decades: A Study of the Arts in America, 1865–1895.* 2nd ed. New York: Dover, 1971.

Nahin, Paul J. *Mrs. Perkins's Electric Quilt and Other Intriguing Stories of Mathematical Physics.* Princeton, NJ: Princeton University Press, 2009.

Neuhart, John, Marilyn Neuhart, and Ray Eames. *Eames Design.* New York: Harry N. Abrams, 1989.

Nye, David. *American Technological Sublime.* Cambridge, MA: MIT Press, 1994.

O'Reilly, Tim. "What Is Web 2.0?" *O'Reilly Media.* http://oreilly.com/web2/archive/what-is-web-20.html.

Ostrow, Stephen. *Digitizing Historical Pictorial Collections for the Internet.* Washington, DC: Council on Library and Information Resources, 1998.

Paasonen, Susanna. *Figures of Fantasy: Internet, Women and Cyberdiscourse.* New York: Peter Lang, 2005.

Palmer, Alexandra. "A Bomb in the Collection: Researching and Exhibiting Early 20th-Century Fashion." In *The Future of the 20th Century: Collecting, Interpreting and Conserving Modern Materials*, edited by Cordelia Rogerson and Paul Garside, 41–47. London: Archetype, 2006.

Pattern Source. Tumblr. http://patternsource.tumblr.com/.

Pearl-McPhee, Stephanie. *Yarn Harlot*. http://www.yarnharlot.ca/.

Pershing, Linda. "She Really Wanted to Be Her Own Woman: Scandalous Sunbonnet Sue." In *Coding in Women's Folk Culture*, edited by Joan Radner, 98–125. Urbana: University of Illinois Press, 1993.

Place, Linna Funk. "The Object as Subject: The Role of Museums and Material Culture in American Studies." *American Quarterly* 26 (1974): 281–91.

Plant, Sadie. "The Future Looms: Weaving, Women and Cybernetics." In *Cyberspace/Cyberbodies/Cyberpunk: Cultures of Technological Embodiment*, edited by Mike Featherstone and Roger Burrows, 45–64. London: Sage, 1995.

———. "On the Matrix: Cyberfeminist Simulations." In *Cultures of Internet: Virtual Spaces, Real Histories, Living Bodies*, edited by R. Shields, 325–36. London: Sage, 1996.

———. *Zeros and Ones: Digital Women and the New Technoculture*. New York: Doubleday, 1997.

Pliny the Elder. *Pliny's Natural History*. Translated by H. Rackham, W. H. S. Jones, and D. E. Eichholz. http://www.masseiana.org/pliny.htm#BOOK%20XXXV.

Poster, Mark. *Information Please: Culture and Politics in the Age of Digital Machines*. Durham, NC: Duke University Press, 2006.

Prown, Jules David, and Kenneth Haltman, eds. *American Artifacts: Essays in Material Culture*. East Lansing: Michigan State University Press, 2000.

Queenan, Joe. "Still Life with Badly Dressed Museum-Goer." *Wall Street Journal*, August 27, 2015. http://www.wsj.com/articles/museums-crack-down-on -your-badly-dressed-visitors-1440691602.

Rabinovitz, Lauren, and Abraham Geil, eds. *Memory Bytes: History, Technology and Digital Culture*. Durham, NC: Duke University Press, 2004.

Redfield, Robert. *The Little Community: Viewpoints for the Study of a Human Whole*. Chicago: University of Chicago Press, 1958.

Rigal, Laura. "Imperial Attractions: Benjamin Franklin's New Experiments of 1751." In *Memory Bytes: History, Technology and Digital Culture*, edited by Lauren Rabinovitz and Abraham Geil, 23–46. Durham, NC: Duke University Press, 2004.

Robertson, Andie. "Interpreting the Woven Devoré Textile." In *The Future of the 20th Century: Collecting, Interpreting and Conserving Modern Material,* edited by Cordelia Rogerson and Paul Garside, 18. London: Archetype, 2006.

Rogerson, Cordelia, and Paul Garside, eds. *The Future of the 20th Century: Collecting, Interpreting and Conserving Modern Materials*. London: Archetype, 2006.

The Rolling Stones. *Exhibitionism*. http://www.stonesexhibitionism.com/exhibi tion/.

Rosales, Vanessa, and Ariele Elia. "Instagram and Fashion." Public lecture given at the Fashion Institute of Technology (FIT) Museum, New York City, October 8, 2015.

Ruskin, John. *Modern Painters*. New York: Effingham Maynard & Co., 1891.

Schreibman, Susan, et al., eds. *A Companion to Digital Humanities*. Oxford: Blackwell, 2004.

Schwarzer, Marjorie. *Riches, Rivals and Radicals: 100 Years of Museums in America*. Washington, DC: American Association of Museums, 2006.

Shakespeare, William. "Song of Spring." *Love's Labours Lost* (1598). http://shakespeare.mit.edu/lll/full.html.

Showalter, Elaine. "Common Threads." In *Sister's Choice: Tradition and Change in American Women's Writing*, edited by Elaine Showalter. New York: Oxford University Press, 1991.

Sikarskie, Amanda Grace. "Erica Wilson and the Quilt Revival." *Uncoverings* 36 (2015): 93–114.

———. "Fiberspace." PhD diss., Michigan State University, 2011.

———. "Living the #Quilt Life: Talking about Quiltmaking on Tumblr." In *Hashtag Publics*, edited by Nathan Rambukkana. New York: Peter Lang, 2015.

———. "Social Media for Quilt History." American Quilt Study Group, Lincoln, NE, October 6, 2012.

Simon, Nina. *Museum 2.0*. http://museumtwo.blogspot.com.

———. *The Participatory Museum*. Santa Cruz, CA: Museum 2.0, 2010.

Singleton, Charles S., ed. *Interpretation: Theory and Practice*. Baltimore: Johns Hopkins University Press, 1969.

Smith, Abby. "Preservation." In *A Companion to Digital Humanities,* edited by Susan Schreibman et al., 576–91. Oxford: Blackwell, 2004.

Smith, Henry Nash. *Virgin Land: The American West as Symbol and Myth*. Cambridge, MA: Harvard University Press, 1950.

Sontag, Susan. *On Photography*. New York: Farrar, Straus and Giroux, 1977.

Sood, Amit. "Building a Museum of Museums on the Web." TED Talks (March 2011). https://www.ted.com/talks/amit_sood_building_a_museum_of_museums_on_the_web?language=en.

Steiner, Frances S. *French Iron Architecture*. Ann Arbor, MI: UMI Research Press, 1984.

Stokstad, Marilyn, and Michael W. Cothren. *Art History*. 5th ed. Boston: Pearson, 2014.

Stott, William. *Documentary Expression and Thirties America*. New York: Oxford University Press, 1973.

Tepper, Steven, and Yang Gao. "Engaging Art: What Counts?" In *Engaging Art: The Next Great Transformation of America's Cultural Life*, edited by Steven Tepper and Bill Ivey, 17–48. London: Routledge, 2008.

Tepper, Steven, and Bill Ivey, eds. *Engaging Art: The Next Great Transformation of America's Cultural Life*. London: Routledge, 2008.

Terras, Melissa. *Digital Images for the Information Professional*. London: Ashgate, 2008.

Tobin, Shelley, Sarah Pepper, and Margaret Willes. *Marriage à la Mode: Three Centuries of Wedding Dresses*. London: The National Trust, 2003.

Toole, Betty Alexandra. *Ada, the Enchantress of Numbers*. Mill Valley, CA: Strawberry Press, 1992.

Tortora, Phyllis, and Keith Eubank. *Survey of Historic Costume*. 3rd ed. New York: Fairchild, 1998.

Trestain, Eileen Jahnke. *Dating Fabrics: A Color Guide*. Paducah, KY: American Quilter's Society, 1998.

Turing, Alan. "Computing Machinery and Intelligence." *Mind* 59 (1950): 433–60.

Turney, Joanna. *The Culture of Knitting*. Oxford: Berg, 2009.

Ulrich, Laurel Thatcher. *The Age of Homespun: Objects and Stories in the Creation of an American Myth*. New York: Alfred A. Knopf, 2001.

———. "Pens and Needles: Documents and Artifacts in Women's History." *Uncoverings* 14 (1993): 221–28.

Venters, Diana, and Elaine Krajenke Ellison. *Mathematical Quilts: No Sewing Required!* Emeryville, CA: Key Curriculum Press, 1999.

———. *More Mathematical Quilts: No Sewing Required!* Emeryville, CA: Key Curriculum Press, 2003.

Vlg-Budde. "Marianne Faithfull Inspired." Polyvore. http://www.polyvore.com/marianne_faithfull_inspired/set?id=112861415.

Voss, Jon. "Radically Open Cultural Heritage Data on the Web." Museums and the Web (2012). http://www.museumsandtheweb.com/mw2012/papers/radically_open_cultural_heritage_data_on_the_w.

Wadewitz, Adrianne. "Wikipedia Is Pushing the Boundaries of Scholarly Practice But the Gender Gap Must Be Addressed." *HASTAC: Humanities, Arts, Science and Technology Alliance and Collaboratory* (April 9, 2013). https://www.hastac.org/blogs/wadewitz/2013/04/09/wikipedia-pushing-boundaries-scholarly-practice-gender-gap-must-be.

Waldvogel, Merikay. *Soft Covers for Hard Times: Quiltmaking and the Great Depression*. Nashville, TN: Rutledge Hill, 1990.

Walker, Alice. "Everyday Use." Crossroads—University of Virginia. http://xroads.virginia.edu/~ug97/quilt/walker.html.

Walsh, Peter. "The Rise and Fall of the Post-Photographic Museum." In *Theorizing Digital Cultural Heritage*, edited by Fiona Cameron and Sarah Kenderdine, 19–34. Cambridge, MA: MIT Press, 2007.

Webster, Marie. *Quilts: Their Story and How to Make Them*. New York: Tudor, 1915.

Weil, Stephen. *Making Museums Matter*. Washington, DC: Smithsonian Institution Press, 2002.

Welter, Barbara. "The Cult of True Womanhood: 1820–1860." In *The American Family in Social-Historical Perspective*, edited by Michael Gordon. New York: St. Martin's Press, 1973.

Weltge, Sigrid Wortmann. *Women's Work: Textile Art from the Bauhaus*. San Francisco: Chronicle Books, 1993.

Williams, Raymond. *Television, Technology and Cultural Form*. New York: Schocken Books, 1974.

Winter, Alison. "A Calculus of Suffering: Ada Lovelace and the Bodily Constraints of Women's Knowledge in Early Victorian England." In *Science Incarnate: Historical Embodiments of Natural Knowledge*, edited by Christopher Lawrence and Steven Shapin, 202. Chicago: University of Chicago Press, 1998.

Woolley, Benjamin. *The Bride of Science: Romance, Reason and Byron's Daughter.* London: Macmillan, 1999.

Wosk, Julie. *Women and the Machine: Representations from the Spinning Wheel to the Electronic Age.* Baltimore: Johns Hopkins University Press, 2001.

Wurtzburger, Wheat, and Anna Kerlin. "Child's Outfit in an Adult Size." Learning to Love You More. http://www.learningtoloveyoumore.com/reports/1/wurtzburger_wheat.php.

Yasko, James. "Museums and Web 2.0." *Museum News* (July/August 2007).

Key Websites

Dublin Core Metadata Initiative, http://dublincore.org.

Flickr Commons, https://www.flickr.com/commons.

Instagram, https://instagram.com.

Linked Data, http://linkeddata.org.

LODLAM, Linked Open Data in Libraries Archives and Museums, http://lodlam.net.

Net-a-Porter, http://www.net-a-porter.com/.

Polvore, http://www.polyvore.com.

Quilt Explorer, http://www.quiltstudy.org/collections/quilt_explorer.html.

Quilt Index, http://www.quiltindex.org/index.php.

Tapestry, http://tapestry.philau.edu.

Tumblr, https://www.tumblr.com.

WGBH Open Vault, http://openvault.wgbh.org.

Wikipedia, https://www.wikipedia.org.

World Quilts: The American Story, http://worldquilts.quiltstudy.org/americanstory/.

Zappos Couture, http://couture.zappos.com.

Index

aesthetic movement, 16, 46
Africa, 46, 47, 49, 54–55
AI. *See* artificial intelligence
AIDS Memorial Quilt. *See* NAMES
    Project
Alcott, Louisa May, 61–62, 101
American Quilt Study Group, 60, 117
Analytical Engine, 5–9, 60, 70, 71,
    118, 127. *See also* Difference
    Engine
animals, depictions in textiles, 17, 46,
    47, 115, 116–17
archives. *See specific archival projects*
Argus, 29
artificial intelligence, xiii, 7, 44, 54,
    63. *See also* social tagging, AI-based
arts and crafts movement, 16, 17, 128
arts participation, hierarchy of, 96
Atget, Eugene, 130, *131*
aura of the work of art, 34, 36–38
authority, curatorial, xii–xiii, 78, 91–
    92, 102–3, 118

Babbage, Charles, 5–7, 9, 60, 67, 118,
    127–28
bargello. *See* embroidery
Baudrillard, Jean, 128
Bauhaus, 120–21

Benjamin, Walter, 34–37
Berlin wool work. *See* embroidery
Berners-Lee, Tim, 71–72
Bicentennial, American, 13, 111, 120
binaries, 1, 4, 6–9, 23, 60, 65, 67,
    69–70, 96, 142
blogs, 58–60, 71, 78, 83–87, 91–92,
    94–96, 99, 103–4
Boileau, Louis-Auguste, 132
Au Bonheur des Dames, 132
Bon Marché, 130, *131*, 131–32, 133
Boucicaut, Aristide, 132
Brackman, Barbara, 14; Brackman
    numbers, 24, 26. *See also* quilts,
    patterns
Brecht, Bertolt, 93
brick-and-mortar world, 13, 19, 23,
    43, 84, 87, 91, 129, 135
Brown, James, 11, *12*, 15, 19, 23
Bruegel the Elder, Pieter, 51, 64
Burton, Sarah, xiii, 141–42
Byron, Annabella, 2, 4, 6
Byzantine art, 82–83

Carnaby Street, 79
Cartland, Barbara, 122, 123
Chessie Kitten, 115, *116*
Child, Julia, 117

children, 4, 17, 59, 61–62, 69, 110,
116–17
Christian, Talula, 85, 86
collections. *See* museums; Polyvore,
collections
collective intelligence, 100
colonialism, British, 49, 142
colonial revival, American, 17, 115,
119
color, xi, 20–21, 24–27, 29, 31, 32,
38, 48–49, 52, 63–65, 79–80,
85–87, 113, 116–17, 120, 123, 142;
in digitization projects, 32; quilt-
specific, 25–27, 51
commodification of history, 108, 128,
135. *See also* historians, professional
compression, lossy and lossless, 32
computers. *See* quilts, computers and
content management, xii, 29, 31
costume, usage as a term, xivn3
Countess of Lovelace. *See* Lovelace,
Ada
Creative Commons, 45
crewelwork. *See* embroidery
crowdsourcing, 66, 102
Cult of Domesticity, 18, 121
curatorial authority. *See* authority,
curatorial
cybernetics: cyborgs and, 66–67;
definition of, 66. *See also* Wiener,
Norbert

database crosswalks, xii, 30–31
data migration. *See* preservation,
migration to new formats
de Certeau, Michel, 91
de Groot, Jerome, 107–8, 128
department stores, 17, 40n16, 130–
32. *See also* shopping, as cultural
pursuit
Design Center, Philadelphia
University, xiii, 51, 55
devoré, *53*, 53–54

Difference Engine, 6, 127. *See also*
Analytical Engine
digital images, xii–xiii, 8, 11, 13, 19,
21, 24, 26, 29–39, 44–46, 48–52,
63, 79, 82–86, 103–4. *See also*
photography, standards for
digitization projects, 21, 32, 38, 109,
111, 113
dress, usage as a term, xivn3
Dresser, Christopher, 46, *47*, 48–49
Dublin Core, 24, 27, 28, 29, 46,
113–14
Duchess of Cambridge. *See* Middleton,
Katherine
dyes, xi, 16, 20–21, 40n15. *See also*
color

Eames, Charles and Ray, 120, 121
Eastlake, Charles, 16
Eco, Umberto, 122, 123
education: moral, 61–62; women
and, 60–61. *See also* mathematics,
women and
Eiffel, Gustave, 132
embroidery, ix, xi, xiii, 17, 29, 108,
111, 113–17, 120, 122–25, 129,
142; bargello, 109, 113; Berlin wool
work, 123, *124–25*; chain stitch,
114, 114–15; cross-stitch, 119, 123,
126; crewelwork, 111, 115, 116,
117, 128; redwork, 17; satin stitch,
123, 124; shisha, 113; turkey work,
109, 115, 117, 123–24; whitework,
117; writing in, 122
Erica (TV program). *See* Wilson, Erica
ethnomathematics, 69–70
ethos. *See* quilts, ethos of; World
Wide Web, ethos of
Exhibitionism (Rolling Stones
exhibition), 107

fabric prints: conversational, 54, 63;
floral, *52*, 53; geometric, *52*, 53

Faithfull, Marianne, 80
Falk and Dierking. *See* museums,
     learning
family: African Americans and, 63;
     dress and, 141; extended, 60;
     hashtags and, 86; heirlooms,
     25, 30, 63; nineteenth-century
     conceptions of, 58–59, 95;
     photographs, 126; privilege and,
     69, 131–32; traditions, 120;
     Victorian, 58–59
fashion: 1960s, 78–80, 84–85, 110,
     123; 1970s, 52, 78, 86–90, 129;
     African American, 79–80, 100;
     usage as a term, xivn3; vintage,
     79–82, 86, 99–100, 102
fashion designers. *See individual*
     designers
Fashion Institute of Technology, 87
Feuerbach, Ludwig, 38
fiberspace, xii, xivn2, 69–70
Flickr Commons, xiii, 45–49, 87
folk culture, 95–96, 98–99, 102; folk
     art and, 38, 94; as opposed to high
     culture, 95, 122
footwear, *125*, 139

gender equity, xiii, 139
gigapixel. *See* Google Art Project;
     photography, gigapixel
Glaspell, Susan, 62
Godey's Lady's Book, 17, 61. *See also*
     magazines
Gombrich, E. H., 119
Google Art Project, 50–51

Hall, Jerry, 87
Halston, 71–72, 79, 87, *88–90*, 91,
     129
Harper's Bazaar, 17, 61. *See also*
     magazines
hashtags, 86–87, 91, 103
Haynes, Luke, 12, 15, 19

Hepburn, Audrey, 77, *78*
high culture. *See* folk culture, as
     opposed to high culture
high-performance computing, 65
historians, professional, 45, 78,
     92, 107–9, 135–36. *See also*
     commodification of history
humachine, 67

Industrial Revolution, 6–7, 16–18,
     121, 128
Instagram, 49–50, 58, 85–87, 91, 95,
     99, 104
International Quilt Study Center &
     Museum, 51
interpretation: definition of, 107–9;
     in relation to other museological
     issues, 22–23, 44

Jacquard, Joseph Marie, 2, 38
Jacquard loom, 2, *4*, 6, 7; punch cards
     for, 1–2, 6, 8, 9, 38, 60, 67, 70, 71,
     128; woven fabric from, 52–53
Jagger, Bianca, 87
Jagger, Jade, 82
jewelry, 82, *83*, 120, 129
July, Miranda, 102

knitting, 70, 71, 84–85
KORA, xii, 29, 30–31
Kruger, Barbara, 129

Lanvin, *134*
Late Age of Print, 118
Learning to Love You More. See July,
     Miranda
Lessig, Lawrence, 94, 101
light, as an agent of deterioration, 19–21
linked data, 45, 71–73
Linked Open Data in Libraries,
     Archives, and Museums
     (LODLAM), 72
little communities, 99–100

Los Angeles County Museum of Art, 46

Lovelace, Ada, xii, xiv, 1, 2, 4–8, *5*, 9, 60, 67, 70, 71, 128

Luddite, xiii, 7, 15, 126, 128

Luna, Donyale, 79–80

Lurex, 120

luxury goods. *See* shopping, as cultural pursuit

Lyons, France, 2, 8

magazines, 17, 18, 61, 79, 126

mail-order catalogs, 17

Marx, Karl, 128

material culture, 9, 13, 16–17, 21–23, 46, 114, 135; definition of, 23

mathematics, women and, 4, 6, 67–70

McQueen, Alexander, xiii, 142

Mellon Participatory Cataloging Project, 110, 113, 117

Menabrea, L. F., 5–6

metadata, xii, 11, 13, 19, 27–31, 45–47, 49–50, 54–55, 82, 87, 110–15, 118; schemes, 13, 23–24, 26, 28–29, 31, 50, 54, 71, 87, 114, 133

Michigan State University, xii, 11, 28–29, 32, 64–65

Middleton, Katherine, xiii, 139–40, 142

Missoni, 79

Miu Miu, 81

Momigliano, Arnaldo, 118

Morris, William, 16, 126

Museum 2.0. *See* Simon, Nina

museums: exhibitions, 11, 16, 22–23, 33–37, 44, 72, 77, 81–83, 86–87, 91, 107–8, 117, 128–29, 133, 135; gift shops, 129; learning, 81–82; photography, 91, 133; virtual visitors, 44; visitors' dress in, 43; on the Web, 50–51. *See also* brick-and-mortar world; object labels; Polyvore, collections

NAMES Project, *37*

National Archives (UK), 46, 47

needlework. *See* embroidery

Net-a-Porter, 79, 135. *See also* shopping

object labels, 80, 87, 104, 119

object records. *See* metadata

obsolete formats, 32, 57

Omeka, 29, 31

online exhibitions. *See* museums, exhibitions; museums, virtual visitors

optical character recognition (OCR), 32

Pallenberg, Anita, 80–81

participatory culture, 94–95, 98–99, 101, 103–4; online, 78, 83, 91–92; scholars and, 110–11

PastPerfect, 29

Philadelphia Centennial Exposition, 14, 16

photography: documentary, 41n55; and family, 126; and fashion, 79; gigapixel, 50; standards for, 31–33; wildlife, 116; and the work of art, 33–36, 39. *See also* digital images; museums, photography

Pinterest, 49, 79, 87

Plant, Sadie, 8, 60, 70

Pliny the Elder, 141

Polyvore, xii, 77, 78–83, 84, 85–86, 92, 93, 96, 102, 103, 104, 128; collections, 77, *78*, 79–82; as shopping site, 79, 108, 128; use in teaching and research, 82

Poster, Mark, 58–59, 67

Potter, Beatrix, 115, 117, 122

preservation: by benign neglect, 21; of digital images, 13, 21, 24, 31–33, 35, 37, 39; migration to new formats, 32; optimization for, 22; and paper records, 11, 13, 30

prints. *See* fabric prints

proto-computer. *See* Analytical Engine

public domain, donation of images and records to, 45–46, 48–49

Quilt Alliance, 19, 21

Quilt Index, ix, xi–xii, 11, *12*, 13, 19, 21–22, *28*, 30–31, 33, 37, 38, 51, 64–65, 139; Comprehensive Fields, 24–29, 31; wiki, 56

quilts: African American, 63, 99; computers and, 15, 126; crazy, 14, 16, 21; documentation projects, 11, 13, 30–31, 33, 38, 41n46; ethos of, 66; of European origin, *28*; literature and, 17, 61–63; patchwork, 17, 61–62, 112–13; patterns, 14, 25–26, 38, 63–64; pictorial, 12, 19; redwork, 17

redwork. *See* embroidery; quilts

resolution, optimal, 31–33

resource description framework (RDF). *See* linked data

retail. *See* shopping

Royal School of Needlework, xiii, 16, 111, 123, 142

Saint Laurent, Yves, 86–87, *88–90*, 91, 129

searches/searchability, xiii, 30, 45, 47, 52, 54–55

sewing: machine, 14–18, 33, 66–67, 126; skills, 14, 18, 95

Shakespeare, William, 34, 122

shisha. *See* embroidery

shopping, 79, 82, 108–9, 128–32, 135, 142; as cultural pursuit, 129–32; online, 108, 133, 135, 142. *See also* department stores; mail-order catalogs; Net-a-Porter; Zappos Couture

silk, xi, *3*, 21, 27, 38, 46, 54, 87, 114, 142; shattering, *22*; weaving, 2, 8

Simon, Nina, 92

Six-Point Manifesto, 103

Le Smoking, 86. *See also* Saint Laurent, Yves

social tagging, xiii, 45–46, 48–49, 53–55, 63, 66, 86–87; AI-based, xiii, 54, 63; languages other than English, 48, 49; scholars and, 111

Sontag, Susan, 34, 39, 77

Sousa, John Philip, 94–95

Spitalfields, 2, 142

steampunk, 127

stitchery. *See* embroidery

style, personal, 77, 80–81

sublime, technological, 57

Sunbonnet Sue, 18

Survey of Public Participation in the Arts, 97

tagging. *See* social tagging

Tapestry, xiii, 51–53, 54–55

technological determinism, 96–97, 99

technology. *See specific technologies*

thrifting. *See* fashion, vintage

triples. *See* linked data

Tumblr, xiii, 49, 77, 78, 83–87, 91, 92, 93, 96, 102, 103, 104

Turing, Alan, 7

Twiggy, 79

Twitter, 58, 86, 87, 104

Ulrich, Laurel Thatcher, 17, 60–61

ultrasuede, 87, *88*. *See also* Halston

user-generated content, 92–93, 100–104. *See also* Lessig, Lawrence; Polyvore; Six-Point Manifesto; Tumblr

Venturi, Robert, 121
Victorian period, 4, 7, 15–17, 46–47, 49, 58–60, 123–28, 142; family, 58–59; revival of, 119–21
virtual visit. *See* museums, virtual visitors
visual stylometry, xiii, 64–66
VRA Core, 24

Walker, Alice, 63, 99
Watteau, Jean-Antoine, 130
Weil, Stephen, 135
weaving. *See* Jacquard loom; silk, weaving
wedding dresses, 141–42; of Katherine Middleton, xiii, 139–40, *140*, 142
WGBH Media Library and Archives, xi, xiii, 108–11, 113–17, 118, 120, 129

whitework. *See* embroidery
Wiener, Norbert, 66. *See also* cybernetics
Wikipedia, xiii, 72, 94, 139–42
Wilson, Erica, xiii, 108–9, 110, 111, 113, 115, 116–17, 119, 120, 122–25, 126, 129, 142
women. *See* education, women and; mathematics, women and; World Wide Web, women and; writing, women and
women's magazines. *See* magazines
World Wide Web: ethos of, 93–94, 100; history, 56–58; semantic Web, 73; theory, 7–8; Web 2.0, 60; women and, 57–58. *See also* participatory culture, online
writing, 5–6, 95, 118; in embroidery, 122; women and, 60–63

Zappos Couture, 135. *See also* shopping
Zola, Émile, 132

About the Author

Amanda Grace Sikarskie is a textile historian, educator, museum practitioner, and blogger whose work investigates material culture—especially textiles—in the digital age. She is currently visiting assistant professor of design history at Kendall College of Art & Design of Ferris State University. Since receiving her PhD in American studies in 2011 from Michigan State University, she has taught undergraduate and graduate-level courses at Kendall College, Michigan State University, and Western Michigan University, including "Museum Technology," "Museum Studies," "Popular Art & Architecture in America," "Design History," "Native Arts of North America," "Historic Preservation," and "Cultural Resource Management." Dr. Sikarskie also holds graduate certificates in museum studies (2008) and humanities computing (2005).

Since 2011, Dr. Sikarskie has been a research associate with the Quilt Index, www.quiltindex.org, an online archive of images and stories for over sixty thousand quilts. Additionally, in 2013, she was a Mellon Scholar with WGBH Boston's Media Library and Archives, working on a participatory cataloging and curation project on *Erica*, an early craft program starring British embroidery guru Erica Wilson that aired from 1971 to 1976. In summer 2014, Dr. Sikarskie was a residential research fellow at the International Quilt Study Center and Museum in Lincoln, Nebraska, conducting work on both Erica Wilson and a collection of peacock appliqué medallion quilts of the 1930s, 1940s, and 1950s.